LAURA AND JIM
AND WHAT THEY TAUGHT ME
ABOUT THE GAP
BETWEEN EDUCATIONAL THEORY
AND PRACTICE

LAURA AND JIM
AND WHAT THEY TAUGHT ME
ABOUT THE GAP
BETWEEN EDUCATIONAL THEORY
AND PRACTICE

Dona M. Kagan

with

James R. Chesnut,
Laura B. Hunter,
C. Beth Burch,
and
Elizabeth K. Wilson

STATE UNIVERSITY OF NEW YORK PRESS

Cover photos courtesy of Commercial Photographic Services,
Tuscaloosa, Alabama

Published by
State University of New York Press,
© 1993 State University of New York

For information, address State University of New York
Press, State University Plaza, Albany, N.Y., 12246

Production by Diane Ganeles
Marketing by Lynne Lekakis

Library of Congress Cataloging-in-Publication Data

Kagan, Dona M., 1946–
    Laura and Jim and what they taught me about the gap between
educational theory and practice / Dona M. Kagan, with James R.
Chesnut ... [et al.].
      p.   cm.
    Includes bibliographical references and index.
    ISBN 0-7914-1544-0. -- ISBN 0-7914-1656-9 (pbk.)
    1. High school teachers--United States--Case studies. 2. College
teachers--United States--Case studies. 3. Teaching--Political
aspects. 4. Teachers--Training of--Political aspects--United
States. 5. Education–United States--Philosophy. I. Chesnut,
James R. II. Title.
LB1777.2.K64   1993
373.11′ 00473--dc20   92-37768
                                                              CIP

10 9 8 7 6 5 4 3 2 1

For my parents,
whose sacrifices allowed me to have
the best education money could buy

And for the many dedicated teachers in Tuscaloosa
with whom it was my privilege to work

CONTENTS

TABLES

TABLES

INTRODUCTION

This is not just a story about two teachers and two professors, it is a story about politics: the politics of teaching. By this I mean the power to define "good" teaching and to decide how new generations of teachers are to be educated. Initially, this power resided in school districts, but it shifted to professors of education, when teaching became a profession legislated by universities.

This transition began in the 1920s and culminated in the 1960s and 1970s when normal schools (teachers colleges) were absorbed into state university systems. Education became a regular university major, and teacher educators assumed the status of university faculty. In order to appreciate the implications of this, one must understand something of university culture and the connotations of "profession" in our society.

As university faculty, teacher educators had a difficult time establishing their credibility and meeting academic norms (Clark, 1987; Labaree, 1992; Wisniewski and Ducharme, 1989), because few were trained to conduct and publish research, the coinage of academe. To justify their status as scholars, teacher educators needed (and continue to need) a scientifically researchable knowledge base: a rational, codifiable body of knowledge with which to build instructional programs of teacher education.

This need is also consistent with our society's perception of a "professional," a status that assumes access to a specialized, technical knowledge base (Labaree, 1992; Schon, 1987; Welker, 1992). That is: to be regarded as true professionals (rather than semiskilled nurturers), teachers needed more than college degrees: they needed to be able to demonstrate acquisition of a *science of teaching* (Labaree, 1992).

Education professors in the subdiscipline of educational psychology were the first and most successful to earn academic credibility, and they did so by generating empirical research closely modeled on the hard sciences: research that was highly rational and positivistic. "Positivistic" describes research that assumes the existence of underlying scientific principles which can be applied to practice to produce predictable results. For the past four decades, the subfield of teacher education has been trying to follow the example set by educational psychology: generating empirical research on classroom teaching/learning that conforms to scientific paradigms, basing teacher education course work on the results of that research.

In short, the credibility of teacher educators (professors of education) is directly related to the promotion of a science of teaching. One can see this clearly in the professional literature: from the individual articles that appear in research journals to the major handbooks regularly published by professional organizations like the American Educational Research Association. This message is also clear in the rhetoric of the Holmes Group, currently the most audible voice calling for greater professionalization of teaching:

> Within the last twenty years. . .the science of education promised by Dewey, Thorndike, and others at the turn of the century, has become more tangible. . .Studies of life in classrooms now make possible some convincing and counterintuitive conclusions about schooling and pupil achievement. Ironically, now that the promise of science of education is about to be fulfilled, many current reform recommendations recall an older literautre that demands a decrease in the time given to the study of this scholarship. (The Holmes Group, 1986, pp. 51–52)

The scientific, rationalized view of classroom teaching promoted by universities and professors is expressed in this book by the two professors you will meet, Beth and Liza. It is a view that I also endorsed, before I began to work closely with teachers and began to see classrooms through their eyes.

Over the past four decades, professors of education (myself included) have worked prodigiously to effect a body of scientific literature, using both quantitative and qualitative methodologies. Indeed, a whole publishing industry of educational research and its applications emerged during the 1970s and continues into the 1990s.

However, what is more remarkable is that practicing teachers have remained virtually impervious to this literature. Once teachers leave their university programs, their pedagogical beliefs and practices are shaped not by research, but by their own classroom experiences and those of fellow teachers. As Cuban (1993) discovered, the classroom practice of most teachers remains as it has been traditionally: teacher-centered and highly structured.

This also describes the classrooms of Laura and Jim, two high school teachers you are about to meet. Their view of teaching reflects the practitioners' perspective, one that is anathema to professors, because it eschews a science of teaching. Instead, Laura and Jim (and other traditional teachers) define teaching as a highly idiosyncratic, individualistic, nonpredictable art of social interaction that is unrelated to the scientific literature of education and educational psychology.

These two conflicting views of teaching are generally referred to by my fellow scholars in terms of differential *cultures* (university, school). However, as I ultimately suggest in this book, explaining the different views in terms of cultures obscures more than it illuminates. Individuals endorse beliefs that have functional value for them. A scientific, rationalized view of teaching justifies the occupation of teacher educators and the existence of university-based programs of teacher education. Without a scientific knowledge base (the professors' perspective), colleges of education no longer possess a warrant to educate novices. If professors of education—like Beth, Liza, and me—eschew the scientific perspective, we put our own professional status in jeopardy.

Sadly, in trying to justify our own role, we have come to monopolize the power to define teaching. In the process of promoting our own functionally valuable perspective, we have disenfranchized experienced practitioners like Laura and Jim, who remain a silent underground of dissenting voices. That is why I made this their story rather than the professors'. One must assume that their perspective also has functional value; namely, it reflects the way classroom teaching is experienced and the way teachers can understand and explain what they do.

Perhaps it is time for teachers to reclaim the right to define and evaluate their profession and to help decide how novices are best prepared for the classroom. It is in this spirit that I invite you to read on.

CHAPTER 1

MOTIVATION AND METHOD

I began to glimpse a subculture among in-service teachers that was not acknowledged by my university colleagues.

In a sense this inquiry began when I first met Jim and we got into a terrific argument. As you will soon discover, Jim teaches eleventh- and twelfth-grade social studies in a high school in downtown Tuscaloosa, Alabama. At the time, I was a faculty member at the University of Alabama in the Department of Curriculum and Instruction, the division that houses the preservice teacher education programs.

The context of our meeting was a joint school-university committee appointed by the university director of student teaching to redesign the forms used to evaluate student teachers. Jim and two other teachers on the committee represented cooperating teachers who regularly hosted student teachers; I was one of three professors representing university faculty who regularly supervised student teachers.

In the course of the committee's initial meeting, Jim delivered an impassioned digression on the "games" a student teacher is forced to play in order to win the approval of his or her university supervisor. Jim was referring to supervisors' habit of requiring student teachers to demonstrate particular instructional strategies, like cooperative learning. According to Jim, these special demonstrations constituted highly artificial disruptions in the normal routine of his classroom.

5

The basis of Jim's objection was twofold: the injection of special lessons impeded his covering the curriculum, and the "cute qames" taught in educational methods courses wasted class time. In Jim's opinion there was only one way to cover the curriculum and that was to address it explicitly. For him that meant "lecture," a term he knew was regarded with derision by education professors like me.

Although Jim said he would not presume to mandate the same style for other social studies teachers, he felt that university supervisors ought to respect the integrity of his classroom. He added that he was happy to share his professional knowledge with student teachers, but that he should not be expected to provide guidance about instructional styles he never used.

I responded to Jim's comments with equal passion, citing the obligation of cooperating teachers to give student teachers chances to practice a variety of instructional models, especially those that are taught in methods courses and are founded on sound theory or research. I added a snide remark about the misguided use of lecture with secondary students.

"Aha," Jim pounced, "that's exactly the attitude I'm talking about!" The pressures placed on cooperating teachers to let their student teachers play games caused him to decide years ago that his student teachers would be limited to only ten days of full-time teaching during their respective placements (the state minimum).

I was outraged by this and said that if I ever supervised a student teacher who was assigned to Jim, I would demand a different cooperating teacher. Surprisingly this did not intimidate Jim, and we continued to argue for the next forty-five minutes as fellow committee members looked on aghast.

The committee met over the subsequent six weeks and eventually accomplished its task of developing evaluation forms acceptable to both school and university personnel. During those six weeks, Jim and I continued our dialogue, albeit with reduced passions. It was the first time in my fourteen years of working in preservice teacher education that an in-service teacher had dared to be so outspoken about his dissatisfaction with university procedures. I had suspected that displeasure existed, but teachers were always too polite or too intimidated to verbalize it.

By the end of the sixth week of dialogue with Jim, a curious thing occurred: I found myself reexamining some of my own very strong beliefs about the role of a cooperating teacher, the role of a university supervisor, and a unilateral definition of "good teaching."

I also began to suspect the existence of an underground, a group of cooperating teachers who adhered to a set of pedagogical beliefs that were diametrically opposed to those espoused by university professors of education. In short, I began to glimpse a subculture among in-service teachers that was not acknowledged by my university colleagues. And I wanted to know more about that subculture.

For example, if those teachers were given the power to restructure student teaching, how would they change it? At the University of Alabama, student teaching was conducted in the traditional manner. That is, each student teacher was assigned to a cooperating teacher and a university supervisor, the latter completing six formal site evaluations and assigning a final grade. What would happen if cooperating teachers were given total responsibility for supervising and evaluating their respective student teachers (i.e., with no university supervisors)? Would the cooperating teachers employ different evaluation criteria or require their student teachers to perform different duties? The subsequent semester my curiosity led to an experiment in which five experienced secondary teachers (of English and social studies, respectively) were given exclusive authority to supervise their own student teachers. Using recommendations of principals and district administrators in the Tuscaloosa City Schools, I identified five cooperating teachers who were scheduled to host student teachers that semester. Each cooperating teacher was described as an outstanding classrooom teacher who had high standards for student teachers and the courage to enforce them. Jim was one of the five cooperating teachers. So was Laura, who teaches English in the same high school as Jim.

Although I served as the university supervisor of record for their student teachers that semester, I made no formal visits or evaluations. Instead the five secondary teachers and I met weekly as a team to discuss the student teachers, compare perceptions, and validate judgments. Those five teachers were to become the first Clinical Master Teachers at the University of Alabama. That term refers to a cadre of outstanding classroom teachers who are granted adjunct faculty status by the university and are empowered to supervise preservice candidates in their field experiences. At the time this is being written, this cadre of teachers has grown to twenty-four.

As I attended the weekly meetings of that first Clinical Master Teacher team and got to know Laura, I discovered that some of her pedagogical beliefs were similar to Jim's. Like Jim, she appeared to endorse a rather traditional, teacher-centered instructional style and was inured to methods professors' versions of "good teaching."

I also learned that Jim and Laura were regarded by colleagues, students, parents, and their principal as outstanding teachers; that Jim had even won a statewide award for best teacher of American history. Both teachers were often given advanced placement classes and, although generally regarded as "hard" teachers, were liked by students who visited between classes to chat. Both teachers were also active in intramural activities: Jim coordinated committees and raised money for the junior/senior prom; Laura sponsored the Scholar Bowl.

How could one explain the seeming contradiction: Jim and Laura were outstanding and popular teachers, yet adhered to instructional styles that are anathema to education professors, particularly those who teach methods courses? This did not represent a new phenomenon to me. In fact, it is a graphic illustration of the notorious "gap between theory and practice": what preservice candidates learn in university course work versus what they see practiced by experienced teachers.

Preservice candidates appear to be particularly sensitive to this gap, for "with regard to the methods and foundations courses, there is much evidence that the knowledge, skills, and dispositions introduced to students in these courses have little influence on their subsequent actions. . ." (Zeichner and Gore, 1990, p. 336).

The implications of research and theory that are so revered by methods professors are generally ignored by in-service teachers (Hall and Loucks, 1982). Instead teachers appear to obtain most of their ideas from actual practice: their own and that of their colleagues (Zahorik, 1987).

This is also true among student teachers who are more influenced by their cooperating teachers than by their university supervisors or course work (Calderhead, 1988; Hoy and Woolfolk, 1989; Zeichner, Tabachnick, and Densmore, 1987). After entering service, teachers continue to solve instructional problems largely by relying on their own beliefs and experiences (Ashton and Webb, 1986; Hoy, 1969; Rosenholtz, 1989: Smylie, 1989).

In this sense teachers appear to develop "practical knowledge" of their craft: knowledge that is situation specific, personally compelling, and oriented toward action (Feiman-Nemser and Floden, 1986). Contemporary research on teacher belief suggests that an effective teacher's practice is rooted in a complex personal pedagogy, a network of beliefs derived from the teacher's personality and thousands of hours of classroom practice (Kagan, 1992).

Long before I met Jim and Laura, I had begun to ask myself: if the instructional methods derived from theory and research represent the most effective teaching strategies, why do so many good teachers eschew them? This question was posed indirectly by Cohen (1991) after studying seven outstanding secondary teachers, each of whom ran tradi-tional, teacher-centered classrooms:

> In the classrooms of these teachers there are a lot of frontal lectures and conventional tests. . . Indeed, though it was not always obvious on the surface, all their classrooms were the very opposite of student-centered. . . Even when students freely interacted with each other, challenged the teacher's remarks, or engaged in guided inquiry, the teacher remained the pivotal figure. . . When there was debate, all

waited for the teacher to deliver the final verdict. (Cohen, 1991, p. 104).

In short, each of the expert teachers Cohen studied failed to correspond to modern notions of good teaching: that is self-directed learning in which the teacher functions more as a resource and facilitator of student-constructed knowledge than an authority.

> ...the overriding goal of their teaching had little to do with student-enablement. They were concerned, rather, with self-enablement—with getting and holding power...Indeed, in every case, the subject's classroom functions as a kind of stage on which a variety of [the teacher's] needs can be asserted and worked through—the need for applause, the need for control, the need for expressing personal talents and interests...In the case of these teachers...student enablement is merely a by-product of the teacher's own pursuit of self-actualization. (Cohen, 1991, p. 105)

This conundrum lies at the heart of this inquiry. After working with Jim and Laura for a year on the Clinical Master Teacher project, I embarked upon an intense analysis of their respective beliefs and classroom practices in hopes of gaining some insight into the gap between theory and practice. The result was this book.

Method and Overview

This inquiry was conducted in four distinct phases that extended over five months, the spring semester of 1992. Each phase is outlined below.

Phase 1

My goal during the first phase was to obtain accurate descriptions of Laura's and Jim's pedagogical beliefs and practices. This included explanations of how each used textbooks, organized and presented academic material, evaluated student learning, designed homework, related to students, and handled class discipline.

I spent twelve hours observing each of them and taking ethnographic field notes. I made a point of observing each teacher in a variety of contexts: presenting different kinds of academic material, presenting the same material to different classes of students, beginning units, and ending units. Each night I typed that day's field notes, often inserting inferences and questions about things I had observed.

After twelve hours of classroom observation extending over a period of five weeks, I used my field notes to construct a narrative description of each teacher.

I gave Laura and Jim copies of their respective narratives and asked them to think about the questions listed below. A week later I obtained their answers via separate ninety-minute interviews:

1. Are any of my observations about your instruction incorrect or misleading?

2. How did you arrive at your present instructional style? What experiences as a student or as a teacher influenced your style? How and why has your style evolved over the years? Has your definition of good teaching changed?

3. What principles or beliefs guide your choice of what you teach and how you teach it?

4. How long have you taught in public schools: what grades/subjects? How have students, classrooms, schools, and teaching changed over those years? What makes you an effective teacher?

5. How did you happen to choose teaching as a career? If one of your own children expressed interest in becoming a teacher, how would you feel?

I audiotaped each interview, transcribed the tapes, and used the transcripts to describe the cognition and values underlying Laura's and Jim's respective practices. My description of what I observed in Laura's classroom, supplemented with the cognition underlying her behavior, appears in chapter 2. The corresponding narrative for Jim appears in chapter 5.

Phase 2

During the second phase I tried to obtain accurate descriptions of the professional beliefs and practices of the university professors who taught corresponding methods courses in the Department of Curriculum and Instruction: Beth Burch, the secondary English specialist; Liza Wilson, the secondary social studies specialist. Each was completing her first year at the University of Alabama. I gave each professor a copy of the questions listed below and interviewed each a week later:

1. Describe your methods course in detail. What do you tell preservice teachers about: selecting, organizing, and presenting academic material; evaluating students; managing a classroom?

2. How did you arrive at your current methods course? What experiences as a student or as a classroom teacher influenced you? Include a description of your background as a classroom teacher. What caused you to leave the public school classroom for a career in higher education?

3. How does the content of your methods course relate to your definition of good English/social studies teaching at the secondary level?

4. In what contexts have you observed secondary English/social studies teachers in Tuscaloosa? How would you evaluate them in general? If you could give teachers one piece of advice, what would it be?

After completing each interview, I gave Beth a copy of the narrative describing Laura's English classes and I gave Liza the corresponding description for Jim's social studies classes. It is important to note that I did *not* give Beth or Liza descriptions of the cognition underlying Laura's or Jim's practices.

I withheld information about cognition for two reasons. First, I wanted to simulate the conditions under which a university professor would usually get to observe and evaluate a classroom teacher. Secondly, I wanted to see what each methods professor might infer from observable classroom practice. Would Beth or Liza leap to any wrong conclusions about why Laura or Jim teach as they do? Would the professors accurately intuit the contextual classroom variables that may have caused Laura and Jim to evolve their respective instructional styles?

A week after giving Beth and Liza descriptions of their respective counterparts, I interviewed each professor again, this time focusing on her evaluation of the classroom teacher. Each of these ninety-minute interviews was audiotaped and transcribed. Chapter 3 contains descriptions of the two interviews conducted with Beth; chapter 6 contains the corresponding descriptions for Liza.

A note about my interviewing technique. It is important here to note the method of interviewing I used with Beth and Liza, when they critiqued the teachers' practices. Each of the professors is sensitive, sympathetic to teachers, and aware of the many constraints imposed upon them. Without provocation, Beth and Liza tended to focus on the positive aspects of their counterparts' practices. Unfortunately, this would serve only to emphasize points of agreement rather than disagreement.

For this reason I assumed a purposely provocative stance during these interviews: often playing devil's advocate and probing the professors' comments for fundamental values. In this sense I did not play the role of a neutral interrogator. Beth and Liza each began by reviewing notes she had made on the written description of Laura's or Jim's practice. I tried to follow each note with broader based questions designed to uncover and examine differences between their perspectives and those of the classroom teachers.

Sometimes I asked Beth or Liza to speculate about the cognition underlying the practice of teachers like Laura and Jim. At other times I drew inferences or generalizations from the professors' comments. Whenever I did so, I stated them explicitly and asked the professors for validation: was this what they meant to say? In describing the interviews, I made a point of preserving the actual texture of our interaction.

Phase 3

During the next phase, I gave a copy of chapter 3 (my interviews with Beth) to Laura; a copy of chapter 6 (my interviews with Liza) to Jim. Now I wanted to obtain the teachers' reactions to the professors' beliefs, methods courses, and critiques of the teachers' practices. I gave the teachers a week to read and digest the respective chapters and then conducted separate interviews with each of them. During each of these 90–120-minute interviews, I asked the following questions:

1. How appropriate is the methods course for preservice teachers? How accurately and usefully does it address the task of teaching secondary English/social studies?

2. If you could give Beth/Liza one piece of advice about her methods course, what would it be?

3. What are the most common strengths/weaknesses of the student teachers with whom you have worked? Do student teachers appear to be getting better or worse (in terms of preparation)?

4. Please react to Beth's/Liza's evaluation of your practice, as it was described by me. Is it fair? Did she misunderstand something about your beliefs?

I audiotaped these interviews, transcribed the tapes, and used the transcripts to write chapters 4 (Laura's response to Beth) and 7 (Jim's response to Liza).

Phase 4

Finally, I used all the data I had gathered (my own field notes, transcripts of my interviews with the professors and the teachers) to draw inferences about the gap between theory and practice: namely, to compare the teachers' and the professors' perspectives.

I supplemented my own insights with those of two student teachers: one who was working with Laura, the other with Jim. I interviewed each student teacher for about an hour, during which I asked the following questions:

1. What (if any) inconsistencies have you noticed between what you were taught in your methods course at the university and what you observed while working with your cooperating teacher?

2. In what ways does Laura's/Jim's classroom practice seem to differ from the principles you learned during your university coursework?

3. What university courses gave you useful information about classroom teaching?

4. When you get your own classes next fall, what methods do you plan to use: those presented in your methods course or those modeled by your cooperating teacher?

Because these student teachers had, in fact, taken their respective methods courses from Beth and Liza, they preferred to remain anonymous, so pseudonyms are used. I audiotaped the interviews and transcribed the tapes.

Armed with my own perceptions and these transcripts, I tried to answer several questions. How did the teachers' and the professors' views of teaching differ and what appeared to cause those differences? How could Laura and Jim be considered outstanding teachers, yet not conform to Beth's or Liza's beliefs? How sensitive to this gap between university and school were the student teachers? My analysis appears in chapter 8.

Before beginning this project each participant was provided with a copy of this introduction. Once data collection began, there was no written or oral communication between the teachers and the professors. As coauthors, each participant (including the student teachers) received and revised successive drafts of the chapters to follow. This means that my descriptions of interviews (audiotapes) were always read and edited by the interviewees.

The Utility of This Project

Readers may wonder why I chose to have the teachers and the professors interact indirectly through me and written texts. Past experience had taught me that teachers are reluctant to criticize professors and often consider even mild disagreement to be impolite. As I mentioned earlier, my experience with Jim's frankness was unique in my fourteen years of practice in higher education. Similarly, I feared that Beth and Liza might censor their respective critiques of the teachers in order to avoid hurting their (the teachers') feelings.

I tried to overcome the reluctance to criticize and confront by buffering direct interaction and by working with two classroom teachers who I felt knew me well enough to risk total honesty. Readers can judge for themselves whether I succeeded in my attempts to obtain honest reactions from all the participants. Again, it is important to stress that each participant was provided with preliminary and final drafts of all the chapters in this book. Changes, corrections, and additions indicated by each participant were incorporated into the final draft.

It is appropriate here to address the value of an inquiry like this: a small case study of two teachers and two methods professors. It is obviously an example of qualitative research, but what may not be so obvious is that it is "qualitative" in the sense that Eisner (1991) uses that term to refer to that which attends to the naturalistic, the interpretive, and the particular.

Its interpretive quality comes from my role as a research instrument. That is, my perceptions and inferences were intended to be integral parts of this inquiry. Given this subjectivity and the extremely narrow scope of this study, readers may question its value: namely, its generalizability to other classroom teachers and methods professors. In the final chapter, I try to assess its generalizability by relating my findings to empirical and theoretical literature on teaching and teacher education. However, I also want to emphasize Eisner's (1991) explanation of knowledge accumulation in the social sciences:

...if knowledge can be said to accumulate, its growth in both education and in the other social sciences is more horizontal than vertical. By horizontal I mean that what we generate through inquiry into educational matters are ideas that contribute to the development or refinement of conceptual frameworks, perspectives, or metaphors through which the world is viewed. We learn...to work with and shift those perspectives, to examine situations from multiple perspectives...[knowledge accumulation] is an expansion of our kit of conceptual tools...Connections have to be built by readers, who must also make generalizations by analogy and extrapolation, not by watertight logic applied to a common language. Problems in the social sciences are more complex than putting the pieces of a puzzle together to create a single, unified picture. Given the diversity of methods, concepts, and theories, it's more a matter of seeing what works, what appears right for particular settings, and creating different perspectives from which the situation can be construed. (Eisner, 1991, pp. 110–11)

In short, knowledge and meaning lie in the eye of the reader, who I trust has the "spectacular capacity to go beyond the information given, to fill in gaps, to generate interpretations, to extrapolate, and to make inferences in order to construe meanings" (Eisner, 1991, p. 211). In this sense I invite each reader to be an active participant in this study, a partner in the investigation, not of "truth," but of meaning.

Acknowledgments

I want to thank Beth and Liza for allowing me to put them in the uncomfortable position of having to evaluate the practices of classroom teaches whom they respect. This was a particularly difficult task for Liza, who admires much of what Jim does with his students.

I am also indebted to Laura and Jim for allowing me to observe and probe their practices. It required great trust and courage, although we had known one another for a year prior to this project. When I first approached them with the idea for this investigation, Laura said she was surprised and flattered that I considered her interesting enough to write about. Jim said he would participate, but as a favor to me: because he liked me and wanted to help me complete this project.

Laura's and Jim's reactions illustrate the tendency of most experienced classroom teachers to diminish their own worth as professionals, their inability to conceive of their practice as expert behavior worthy of close study. How could anyone, especially a university professor, find their teaching interesting enough to write a book about it? Above all, I hope that this project allowed Laura and Jim to see their teaching in a new light, to understand how it evolved, and to appreciate the expertise they have acquired from long practice, talent, and intuition.

How This is a Different Kind of Educational Research

This inquiry is not educational research in the traditional sense of a theory-driven outsider view of classrooms and teaching. Instead it reflects a "primary concern with describing social events and processes in detail and a distaste for theories which. . . ride roughshod over the complexity of the social world" (Day, 1991, p. 538). It is also in the tradition of practitioner/teacher research in that it represents, in part, an attempt to help Laura and Jim make visible the craft the underlies their practices (Carr and Kemmis, 1986: Lytle and Cochran-Smith, 1991).

This inquiry is also based on the assumption that it is in the "lived situations of actual children and teachers. . . that the teaching enterprise exists and can best be understood" (Ayers, 1992, p. 152). Schubert and Ayers (1992) call this kind of narrative "teacher lore," the stories of teachers and their lives that constitute the natural history of teaching.

Readers will see that in order to explain Laura's and Jim's practices I had to examine biographical details of their lives because the unique trajectories of Laura's and Jim's lives greatly influenced the professional roles they chose to play. To truly understand what these teachers do and why they do it, one must understand the unique set of circumstances that brought each of them to a classroom in Central High in the spring of 1992.

The School Context

Which brings us to the school context. Let me set the scene before I introduce Laura and Jim.

Although there are two high schools in Tuscaloosa, they are regarded as two campuses of one school: Central High. The West campus houses all ninth and tenth graders in the district; the East campus, where Laura and Jim work, houses all eleventh and twelfth graders. This rather strange arrangement is an artifact of court-ordered integration dating back twenty years.

The student body on the East campus numbers about 1,150, 55 percent of whom are black. In some ways Central High is typical of other inner-city schools, but in other ways it isn't. It is a large, lively center of activity located in the heart of a business district. It appears to draw students from a wide range of socioeconomic backgrounds. About 80 percent graduate and go on to two- or four-year colleges or technical schools.

Student teachers have told me that if one looks closely, one can find evidence at Central of the same ills that plague inner-city schools throughout the United States: student gangs, drugs, racial tension. However, none of these factors are obvious nor do they dominate life at Central. Incidents of violence among students are rare. The few instances of which I am aware occurred after hours on school grounds but not inside the school itself. I have never heard of any physical confrontations between students and teachers.

Indeed, most of the teachers appear to maintain exceptionally warm and relaxed relationships with their students. As one walks down the corridors of Central, classes are orderly and apparently on task; one assumes teaching and learning are taking place. Students, black or white, seem to possess school spirit and support social and athletic events. One cannot spot obviously burnt-out or unhappy teachers, although it would be naive to assume none exist among a faculty of seventy.

To someone like me, who grew up and attended high school in a suburb of New York City, the atmosphere at Central seems decidedly relaxed. The principal is regarded by my colleagues at the university as young, bright, and progressive. He appears to be supportive of and well-liked by the majority of his faculty; at least I have never heard teachers speak of him in other than positive terms. In sum, as inner-city schools in the 1990s go, Central High seems to be a pleasant place for both students and teachers.

CHAPTER 2

WHAT I SAW
IN LAURA'S CLASSROOM

They don't need to spend time taking another class or paying a tutor, because I didn't teach them these skills. There's no limit to what these children can do, if you give them the right springboard.

Laura is a petite blond with a consistently cheerful classroom personality. In the twelve hours I sat in her classroom, I never once saw her enthusiasm flag, not even in the face of students' apathy and grossly deficient skills. She's one of the few women I've known who qualifies for the adjective "perky."

Laura begins every class with humor: "Well, has everyone finally recovered from the weekend?" or "I'm glad you all decided to come back after yesterday's test. What did you think of it—a real killer, right? But look who survived!" "Hello, everyone, how's your Monday?"

During the spring of 1992 Laura had three preparations, all at the eleventh grade: advanced composition (two classes), regular composition (one class), and American literature (two classes). This schedule represented a wide range of student ability as well as academic content. I spent equal amounts of time observing each class over a five-week period.

Advanced Composition

Although advanced composition is regarded as a precursor to advanced placement English (twelfth grade), criteria for enrollment are loose. Students are expected to have an overall B average and the recommendations of last year's English teachers. However, students who do not meet those criteria but who have insistent parents cannot be barred from the course. Each of the two advanced composition classes was relatively small: rarely more than twenty in attendance, about 20 percent black. I did not notice significant differences between the two advanced composition classes in terms of Laura's instructional style or the students' skills.

The content of this course includes relatively sophisticated grammatical structures of English: how to identify and label their subcomponents, how to use and punctuate them correctly. Much of the material is complex and technical, including gerundive, participial, and infinitive phrases/clauses and the different ways writers can deploy them to construct varied sentences.

Laura explains to her students that the purpose of learning this material is twofold: to help them write sophisticated prose and to prepare them for college entrance exams. Students in both advanced classes were clearly academically motivated and college bound, and Laura repeatedly reminded them of the latter objective.

In all the classes I observed Laura moved quickly, and the students remained focused and responsive, readily volunteering answers to her questions and admitting when they did not understand. Laura never had to discipline students in these classes or even call them to attention. Lessons generally followed a standard format: first Laura would allude to what was covered in the prior lesson; she would then preview the upcoming lesson via an outline or leading questions written on the blackboard; she might call for questions on last night's homework; and, finally, she would begin the new material. Most of the time she worked with students as a whole class, although she occasionally asked them to compare completed homework assignments in small groups.

In the very first class I observed, Laura explained to students that they would be spending the first six weeks of the course acquiring a common "informational foundation" of grammar which they would then learn to use in the remainder of the course. "It's like learning your multiplication tables in math," she explained. "Then you continue to use that knowledge later in solving problems."

In specific terms, Laura's approach to teaching composition could be described as follows: she begins by introducing students to complex subordinate structures, which they learn to identify and parse; students then complete exercises requiring them to create the structures by combining or modifying short sentences; students then generate their own complex sentences following specific patterns. In the final six weeks of the course (which I did not observe), students practice using complex sentences to create paragraphs and complete essays. During that time Laura also introduces them to the process of writing a research paper, their final and largest assignment in the course.

I heard her describe this pedagogical approach to writing to a student as follows: "I'm asking you to learn how to build new houses [write original sentences, paragraphs, essays] using blueprints that I give you. You have to learn how to choose your own wallpaper and paint, but underneath, the structure of your house must match my blueprint."

All of my observations took place during the first part of the course, when Laura was familiarizing her students with sophisticated grammatical structures and asking them to generate sentences that followed particular patterns. Her focus was on the organization and explication of highly technical material. She appeared to take full responsibility for defining, organizing, and transforming the content into a set of class notes.

Her primary organizational tools were outlines and lists that she wrote on the blackboard or on transparencies. Occasionally she directed students to copy particular rules or examples into their notes, usually reminding them this was important material likely to appear on a test.

Although Laura dominated conversation in both advanced composition classes (doing about 60–70 percent of the speaking), she did not lecture. One could best describe her style as a dialogue with students, as she asked questions requiring them to reason inductively. She used many examples and illustrations to help students arrive at correct answers, often leading them through step-by-step solutions. Her emphasis on inductive logic reinforced the linear arrangement of content.

In addition to using examples and illustrations, she made creative use of metaphors and tried to relate material to the students' everyday lives. As I watched her in these classes, I got the sense that she was working from a detailed "map": she always knew exactly where she was going and how each piece of the lesson fit into the whole curriculum. I never saw her pause, backtrack, or lose her place.

Although Laura's tone is brisk and businesslike (she utilizes every bit of a sixty-minute period), she also jokes and banters with students. When a student gives a correct answer, she often shakes his or her hand: "Good job. Miss _____." She is also honest in acknowledging the differences between oral and written sentence structures: the informal and formal versions of English.

When only one or two students in a class fail to catch on, she invites them to help sessions after school rather than slowing the pace of the day's lesson. What follows are selected portions (verbatim) of two lessons I observed. Each illustrates the characteristics of Laura's instructional style that I have summarized above:

> [Before class began, Laura wrote the objectives of the new unit on the blackboard: recognize verbals; write sentences effectively using verbals; write sentences patterned after American authors.]
>
> **Laura:** We're going to look at the most common mistakes associated with verbals and learn how to correct them. We'll practice writing sentences and then learn to pattern our own sentences after outstanding authors. This will help you avoid always writing simple sentences. Find a place in your

notebook to begin the new unit. Now, tell me what you know about verbals.

[Students volunteer information about gerunds, participles, and infinitives that they have already learned. Laura then dictates a standard definition for "verbal" and writes two terms on the blackboard: "finite verbs," "nonfinite verbs. "]

Laura: What do you know about the words, finite, and nonfinite? What other terms or subjects come to mind?

Student: Science.

Laura: Yes, finite has to do with boundaries and confinements. Let's look at the study sheet I handed out yesterday. Let's begin reading under "verbals."

[Laura calls on individual students who read portions of the study sheet which defines and illustrates finite and nonfinite verbals. Laura then goes to the blackboard and writes the word, "cooking." She explains that cooking is a nonfinite verb because, with a helper, it can serve as a predicate: for example "is cooking."]

Laura: Cooking is a nonfinite verbal. It has characteristics of a verb but not enough to make it a predicate. It can also be a noun. The point is that something is missing that prevents it from ever being a predicate verb. Put this in your notes: Any sentence that contains a nonfinite verb must also contain a finite verb.

[She asks several students to read the rule back to her to make sure they have copied it correctly. She stresses that this is an important concept that should be coded as such in the class notes. She asks students to suggest how this might be accomplished. They suggest using an asterisk or different colored ink.]

Laura: If you know this rule, you won't make mistakes. Now let's test your logic. Is the following statement true or false: If a sentence contains a nonfinite verb, it must also contain a finite verb; therefore, all sentences that contain finite verbs must also contain nonfinite verbs.

[Students agree this is a false statement and explain why.]

Laura: Good. Are we ready to leave these two terms? O.K., let's do some outlining now.

[Laura writes the following on the blackboard:

VERBALS

Types of verbals

I. Gerund

    A. Verb qualities

    B. Noun qualities

As she writes, she points out that this is a topic outline, which is why she is capitalizing only the first word in each line. The class had learned about topic outlines in the tenth grade. Laura stops writing and asks students to suggest verb and noun qualities of gerunds. They indicate they are not sure what she means, so she resorts to a metaphor.]

Laura: Think about Halloween when kids get dressed up and go trick-or-treating. Let's pretend I'm a verb who wants to go trick-or-treating but needs a costume. Would I come to your door dressed as a verb? No, I might come dressed as a noun. [Here Laura actually puts on a face mask that she has brought in for this lesson.] See, now I'm a verb in a disguise, dressed in noun clothing. A verb can come to your home on Halloween dressed as a noun, an adjective, or an adverb. But take his costume away, and he's a verb. There's something missing that would allow him to be a true verb. Imagine that the something missing is his mother (the helping verb) who stands out by the streetlamp while he knocks on your door. The main verb must always accompany the disguised verb (the gerund).

[Laura now enters the following material on the blackboard:

    A. Verb qualities

      — ends in "ing"

        (derivational ending)

      — has adverbial modifiers

    B. Noun qualities

      — has adjective modifiers

      — can be in any noun's position

She asks students to give her examples of gerunds disguised as nouns or verbs. They are stumped, so she proceeds to write examples on the board:

Cooking pizza for the class consumed Mary's time.

Laura asks the students to identify the gerund and each component in the gerundive phrase. After they do this correctly, she writes two more sentences on the board to illustrate how a possessive form of a noun or pronoun can be used to modify a gerund:

Her cooking pizza for everyone was a generous act.
Mary's cooking pizza was a generous act.

Laura asks if there are any questions. When there appear to be none, she asks students to take out the information sheet she had given them the day before. It includes rules about using gerunds and an exercise requring students to rewrite sentences, inserting possessive modifiers before gerunds. After going over some of the sentences together, Laura writes the following on the blackboard:

The President objected to us arriving.

Laura: Is that correct? No, he wasn't upset with *us* but with our arrival. That is a common mistake people make with gerundive phrases. Do you see the logic in it? Let's try one more. . . .

[After working through another example, Laura assigns a similar exercise for homework.]

Two days later students are beginning to write sentences that conform to particular patterns. Laura distributes two sheets: a "fact sheet" listing mistakes to avoid in writing verbals and a writing activity. The writing activity consists of seven sentences, each taken from a famous American author. In each sentence, verbal phrases/clauses have been broken away from the main clause. Students must parse the structure of each sentence then write an original sentence with a similar structure.

The structures are quite sophisticated. One sentence, attributed to Faulkner, reads: "He sat on a log, the invisible compass in his hand." After students analyze the structure correctly, one student dictates a matching sentence: "I ran toward the woods, an enormous officer on my heels." Laura then tries to summarize the process of creating an original sentence:

> **Laura:** Start building from your predicate verb. Then find a subject that logically goes with the verb. Finally, add your descriptive phrases. If you go through this process with each sentence, you will begin to appreciate the artistry of words. Yes, I know it's hard. So far you have just listened and regurgitated: now you have to think.

> [The remaining sentences are assigned for homework. Laura distributes another information sheet introducing a new grammatical structure, absolutes.]

> **Laura:** Today we're going to look at a different structure. Has anyone ever encountered absolutes before? Anyone ever studied Latin? [Two students nod, yes.] Let's all turn to p. 384 of your grammar text and begin with the definition of an absolute. Steve, please read it aloud. [After Steve reads it, Laura repeats it.] An absolute phrase is dramatically different from the rest of the sentence. It often consists of a noun that serves as the subject plus a participle.

> [Laura writes two short sentences on the blackboard:

> > The pony raced across the meadow.
> > His mane was flying in the wind.]

> **Laura:** Now, let's take those two ideas and create a single sentence. [Students dictate several options, and Laura writes one on the blackboard: "The pony, his mane flying in the wind, raced across the meadow."] What does the descriptive factor modify? [Students respond.] "Flying" is a participial form of the verb, right? Remember our discussion on finite and nonfinite verbs a few days ago? This phrase tells me not only the action but what's doing the participial activity: the mane. O.K., let's write this rule in our notes: If the doer of the participle's activity precedes the participle, the structure becomes an absolute construction. Now, there are two points to note about absolutes. An absolute is separated from the rest of the sentence by a comma, and the idea of the absolute must be closely

related to the main clause. Got that? Now let's see where these things come from.

[Laura turns to the board and writes three sentences:

A child sat on the log beside a creek.
Her toes were touching the warm sand. Her eyes were staring into the forest.]

Laura: Can anyone comment about relationships among these sentences? [One student points out which is the most important. Another points out that the other two are parallel and descriptive.] Now, how am I going to make this a single sentence?

[Together, Laura and the students arrive at two possible sentences which she writes on the board:

The child sat on the log beside the creek with her toes touching the warm sand and her eyes staring into the forest.

The child sat on the log beside the creek, her toes touching the warm sand, her eyes staring into the forest.]

Laura: Which sentence do you like best? [Students indicate the second.] Jackie, tell me what I did to create that new sentence. [The student haltingly reviews the steps.] Right, I took out the part of the verb that made it a predicate verb and added a participial ending instead. What did I do with the doers? Nothing. I left them. And what did I create? [Students answer in unison: an absolute.] Yes, because I have a doer (eyes, toes), the absolute construction (staring, touching), and in order to help the reader, I added two commas. Look how graphic that new sentence is. If you want the reader to visualize an image, you need to use an absolute construction. More specifically, this is a "cumulative absolute sentence."

[Here Laura stops and distributes another writing activity. It consists of a descriptive paragraph containing relatively simple sentences. Students are to turn the paragraph into five absolute sentences for homework. Laura points out that in real life one would not want to put so many absolutes together in a single paragraph, but this is just for practice.

She and the students spend some time reviewing the steps involved in creating absolute constructions.]

Laura: Let me tell you something, and it isn't rumor—it's fact. I know that next year in AP English, Mr. M. will ask his students to write "an absolute construction" at a particular point in a paragraph. He isn't going to define what he means, and each one of you who goes on into his class will be able to do what he asks, right?

[For the remainder of the period, Laura and the students work on combining short sentences into single sentences with absolute constructions. At the end of the series, a long absolute construction remains written on the blackboard.]

Laura: What kind of sentence needs to come next, if we were writing a paragraph? [No response.] Well, a complex or a simple sentence? Yes, a short, simple one for contrast. Remember when we read Steinbeck, how he began with a broad panoramic view of the landscape and then began to focus on details until he reached a single ear of corn. That's a good illustration of how the length and complexity of sentences can be varied effectively within a paragraph.

At this point I could see what lay ahead: familiarizing students with the structures of paragraphs and giving them practice generating original paragraphs that conform to particular patterns.

Regular Composition

Laura's regular composition class follows a similar curriculum, except the grammatical content and writing tasks are simpler. Laura's presentation is also different: slower, more explicit, punctuated with frequent repetition. As she does in her advanced classes, Laura assumes full responsibility for organizing the content and dictating class notes.

However, the greatest difference between the advanced and regular classes is the nature of the students. Where those in the advanced classes appeared to be academically able and responsive, most students in the regular composition class demonstrated difficulty mastering the material and rarely volunteered answers to Laura's questions. Because her questions were usually met with silence or whole-class responses, it was impossible to determine how successfully she communicated content.

Attendance rarely fell below twenty-five students, 30 percent of whom were black. Since no advanced placement college entrance test loomed on the horizon for these students, the only concrete motivation to master material was to earn good grades. To make matters worse, the class was taught in two thirty-minute sections divided by a brief lunch period. Nevertheless, Laura did not have to administer serious discipline at any time. She remained cheerful, relaxed, and intimate as she bantered with the students.

The following verbatim excerpt illustrates Laura's efforts to make the material accessible to her students. It also captures the unresponsive nature of the students:

[Laura displayed a transparency that illustrated how to punctuate adverbial clauses. It began with two sentences:

—— *If the coat is too long,* we can shorten it.

—— We can shorten the coat *if it is too long.*

Below these sentences Laura listed several rules. She reads them aloud and instructs the students to copy them into their notes:

1. An introductory adverbial clause is set off with a comma.

2. In order to make a main idea more effective or dramatic, place the adverbial clause at the beginning of the sentence.

Laura walks around the classroom making sure that students are copying this accurately. She identifies several students who are not taking notes and admonishes them lightly. Then she asks the students to turn to a particular page in their grammar texts and directs a girl to read aloud. Laura interrupts occasionally to emphasize an important point. She asks two other students to reread the same section aloud. Finally, she repeats one of the sentences herself.]

Laura: "An adverb clause that follows a main clause is usually not set off by a comma." Do we all understand when to set off the clause with a comma and when not to use a comma? [No response.]

[She displays another transparency:

THE USE OF THE PERIODIC SENTENCE
FOR EMPHASIS

A periodic sentence withholds its main idea until the end: a loose sentence begins with the main idea and ends with subordinate details. A skillful periodic sentence is therefore dramatic; it creates suspense.

Several sample sentences are listed on the transparency. Laura reads each aloud and reminds students to copy them carefully into their notes.]

Laura: There's an easy way to remember the definition of a periodic sentence: "periodic sentence—main idea by the period." Jay, what's an easy way to remember the definition of a periodic sentence? [Jay repeats it, and Laura calls on two more students to repeat the mnemonic.] O.K., now you'll need to know that for the test. Why do you suppose we write periodic rather than loose sentences? [No answer.] To emphasize. Let's look at the examples listed on the transparency. [She reads them aloud.] We use the periodic sentence for what reason, Larry? [He answers correctly.] And, Mary, what is the definition of a periodic sentence? [Mary reads from her notes.]

[Laura asks the students to turn to a page in their grammar texts that lists subordinating conjunctions and an exercise for creating periodic sentences with adverbial clauses. She leads them through the first sentence.]

Laura: What do I do first? [No response.] The first thing I do is look at the two short sentences and decide what the relationship is between them. And what is it in the first sentence? [No response, so Laura gives the answer.] Now give me a subordinating conjunction that expresses that relationship. [One student calls out an answer, which Laura

uses to construct a new sentence.] Let's write these steps
on the board. [Laura writes:

1. Decide on the relationship
2. Decide on whether you will write a loose or
   periodic sentence
3. Decide on punctuation

Example: Take a camera and a notebook on any
trip.
You can record your impressions on
film and on paper.]

Laura: Which is the main idea? [One student calls out the
correct answer.] O.K., then we need to put that in the
independent clause. Where does the subordinating conjunction go? Before which clause? [A student says, "The
dependent. "] The dependent, right. Now, let's make it
periodic. Where does the main idea come? [A student
suggests, first.] What does that tell us about the punctuation? And what should we use for a subordinating
conjunction? [Several students call out answers, and Laura
writes the new sentence: "Take a camera and notebook on
any trip so that you can record your impressions on film
and paper."] Let's do the rest of the exercise for homework.
You decide whether to make periodic or loose sentences,
but you must label each. Try to write three loose and two
periodic.

American Literature

The curriculum of Laura's American literature classes is
typical of all high school survey courses bearing that name:
that is, it presents a highly simplified and condensed overview
of American literature from the colonial period to the early
twentieth century, hitting the usual highlights (Washington
Irving, Poe, Hawthorne, the muckrakers of the late nineteenth
century). Every author and literary work is placed in its
historical and sociological context.

The interesting thing about Laura's American literature
classes was the semiliterate nature of the students and the
ways she managed to adapt the curriculum to their minimal

skills. It constituted quite a challenge, considering the difficulty of the prose and the amount of historical background. In fact, I doubt that I could have imagined how to do it before observing Laura.

Attendance in each class was usually about twenty students, 70–75 percent of whom were black. With perhaps one exception per class, the students were apathetic and inarticulate. When forced to respond, they usually spoke in two- or three-word phrases rather than complete sentences. For the most part Laura wound up answering her own questions and doing 99 percent of the talking. When asked to read aloud from handouts or the textbook, students read slowly, groping along as if they were translating from the Latin. I would guess that the average reading level in each class was fifth or sixth grade.

Laura used a number of techniques to adapt the content and make it accessible. First, she never assumed that students completed or comprehended assigned reading; all the information presented in text was repeated orally in class and dictated into class notes. When providing this information, Laura spoke slowly, simply, and with much repetition. She broke everything down into small steps, which she frequently summarized and asked students to repeat aloud.

Her speech was reinforced with transparencies that organized and condensed information needed for tests. When students were supposed to be copying notes from a transparency, Laura walked around the class, peeking over shoulders to make sure they were following directions. She also tried to relate material to students' daily lives, often using humorous examples.

In sum, she treated these high school juniors like sixth graders, yet there was never a trace of condescension or impatience in her demeanor. She was consistently cheerful and joked intimately with individuals. She moved at a relatively quick pace, using every second of these classes. If the bell marking the end of a period were delayed, she would instruct students to read aloud from the textbook or begin a homework assignment.

Despite Laura's many attempts to relate material to students' lives and to elicit interest, they remained apathetic and unresponsive. The single exception to this that I observed was part of a lesson on life in colonial America, when Laura compared the daily life of a Puritan woman to that of a contemporary woman:

> **Laura:** Who can tell me what the life of the typical Puritan woman was like? [No response.] Well, where did she get food for her family? [No response.] Did she go to the super-market? Were there stores like _____? [Here Laura names some local supermarket chains and the students laugh.] And where did she get clothing for her family? [No response.] Did she go to department stores like _____? [Laura names some local stores, and the students laugh again.] How do you think a wife behaved at home in relation to her husband? Were women educated? [At this point several boys suggest that colonial women had to obey their husbands. The class erupts in laughter, as the girls call out comments like, "No way, man."]

The following verbatim excerpt, taken from a lesson introducing the unit on Romanticism, captures Laura's instructional style in these classes:

> [Laura begins by displaying a transparency:
>
> *Native Grounds*
>
> 1800–1840
>
> Romanticism
>
> | *Characteristics* | *Major Writers* |
> |---|---|
> | love of nature | Irving |
> | focus on self | Cooper |
> | supernatural | Bryant |
> | exotic | Poe |
> | idealism | |
> | nationalism | |
>
> She instructs the students to copy the transparency into their notes.]

Laura: Tomorrow is Valentine's Day, but that's not the kind of romanticism we're going to talk about. We're going to study four writers: Poe, Washington Irving, Bryant, and Cooper. We'll start with Cooper tomorrow. Now let's look at the characteristics of Romantic literature. [She reads aloud from the transparency.] As we study each writer, we're going to look for each of these characteristics. Did any of you see the movie, *The Legend of Sleepy Hollow?* That's a story by Washington Irving. Are you familiar with any of these other authors? [No response. At this point Laura introduces the filmstrip on Romanticism that the class is about to watch.]

Laura: Now, I didn't make a list of study questions for this filmstrip, but from time to time we'll stop to make sure we're putting important points in our notes.

[The filmstrip begins. After every other frame, Laura calls on a student to regurgitate information just narrated.]

Laura: [repeating the narrator] Knickerbocker was one of Irving's pen names. So was Jeffrey Crayon. Do you know of any other writers who use pen names?

Student: Samuel Clemens.

Laura: Yes, good. Lisa, what was one of Washington Irving's pen names? [Lisa repeats, Jeffrey Crayon.]

[The narrator of the film strip states that, "The center of literary life was New York."]

Laura: What do you think that means?

Student: That it was crowded there?

Laura: No, that's where most writers worked, in New York. Be sure to put that in your notes.

[Later, after the last frame on Washington Irving, Laura pauses to summarize.]

Laura: So, who became our first internationally recognized author? [A student calls out, "Washington Irving."] Yes, Washington Irving. Do we all have that in our notes?

Student: Why did they write under different names?

Laura: Sometimes to protect themselves. Society didn't really approve of writers. O.K., let's go on now and hear about Cooper.

[After the section about Cooper, Laura again pauses to summarize.]

Laura: What does Cooper write about? [No response.] Past history. Put it in your notes. Cooper created what came to be our first literary hero. You were supposed to read about him last night in your textbook. Do you remember his name? [It was just mentioned on the film strip, but there is no response.] No? Well, it was Natty Bumppo: N-A-T-T-Y B-U-M-P-P-O. Natty Bumppo was our first literary hero. He had all the characteristics of heroes today. Sometimes he was called "Deerslayer." Now, I've taken a description from *The Deerslayer* which describes our hero. For homework I want you to read it and complete this worksheet. [Laura now distributes two sheets: one with the description, the other with two columns, "Natty Bumppo," "Your Hero."] On the worksheet you will see two columns. In the first column I want you to list the characteristics of Natty Bumppo that make him a hero. In the other column I want you to list the characteristics of your hero. Make it a fictional hero. Alicia, what is our homework assignment? [Student repeats it.] And, Lisa, what is our homework assignment? [Student repeats it again.] Right. Read the description first. Then list the characteristics of each hero. Bring the sheets to class tomorrow, so we can work with them.

[Laura finishes the filmstrip, pausing about every other frame to review.]

Laura's Most Characteristic Strategies

I was able to identify several aspects of Laura's teaching style that appeared consistently in classes, regardless of the curriculum or the students. One was the role she assumed: information giver and organizer. She dictated class notes, using outlines and lists written on the blackboard or on transparencies.

Another pervasive characteristic was her cheerfulness and enthusiasm, both of which appeared to be as genuine in regular classes as they were in the advanced classes. To help translate material, she used examples, comparisons, and metaphors. Whenever possible, she related parts of her lessons to events occurring in students' lives.

Motivation to learn was to do well on tests, but Laura never threatened students with tests; rather, she seemed to be doing everything within her power to help students obtain high scores. That is, she presented herself as an advocate rather than a protagonist.

In every class she maintained a brisk, businesslike pace and used every second for instruction; she left no vacuums during which students could become boisterous. On the rare occasions she needed to discipline students, she did so privately and with a light, feminine tone. Even in the most apathetic classes, she demonstrated affection for her students, engaging them in good-natured bantering and teasing. It is interesting to note that these appeared to be typical inner-city teens, and some of the boys were twice her size. Yet, during the hours I observed her classes, I saw no student confront Laura, express hostility, or refuse to conform to class rules.

Loose Ends

When I finished writing this description of Laura's classroom practice, I knew it was incomplete. The longer I observed her, the more I realized I was not seeing the whole picture. It took five hours of observation before I even began to perceive patterns underlying her teaching. There were many unanswered questions:

1. The content of her advanced composition course was so difficult, did students really understand and integrate it into their own writing? After one of her advanced classes, I was amazed to see a boy approach Laura with a novel by Tolstoy (in translation) and indicate a portion of prose that

illustrated a grammatical structure they had just discussed in class. Surely he was atypical (?).

2. Did the students in her American literature classes really need to learn this material? Whom did Laura blame for these students' grossly deficient reading and writing skills? What does she see herself realistically accomplishing with these students?

3. How could she endure the apathy and unresponsiveness of the students in American literature and remain so cheerful? How was she able to sustain her patience and enthusiasm? Was she putting on an act?

With these and other questions in mind, I gave Laura a copy of this narrative and a list of questions designed to elicit the cognition underlying her teaching and factors that may have influenced her style (see Chapter 1 for the questions). A week later I conducted a two-hour interview with her, during which she attempted to answer those questions.

The Cognition Underlying Laura's Practice

I met Laura in her classroom after school and began the interview by asking her how she had arrived at her present style of teaching English. In response, she described three teachers who had influenced her. One was a "straightlaced grammarian" who used exercises and drills, requiring students to regurgitate information. The second was a junior high school teacher who outlined content on the blackboard and managed to teach note-taking skills covertly. The third was a high school science teacher:

"He taught everything from the core out. You learned a concept and then saw how it gradually evolved into increasingly larger concepts." Later, Laura would remember that technique for her own students: "It seemed a good way to teach children that if they took a kernel sentence and expanded it, they could develop a paragraph. If they took the core of a good paragraph and expanded it, they could get an essay. From there they could get chapters and dissertations.

Basically I teach that structures can be expanded and used for something larger."

Although Laura began by patterning her teaching after the grammarian, she knew her material so well that she was soon able to modify it so learning grammar became more of a "logical, deductive thinking process."

Laura came to teaching by a combination of accident and economic necessity: "I became a teacher, because I was a simple child living in the country. In my generation I had the options of becoming a nurse, a secretary, or a teacher." She was put off by the gore of medicine and knew she couldn't be a secretary, because she couldn't sit still that long. "My energy level doesn't allow me to sit at a desk." So she turned to the only remaining alternative: teaching.

However, she admits that she may have been influenced by her experience teaching piano in high school. "Basically I went into teaching because I desperately wanted to go to college, and by majoring in education I could get grants that would pay my tuition. I had no money, and there were no other ways to get grants in those days."

With a National Defense Education Act loan she began her college years by preparing for a career teaching music. She switched to English when she discovered that the loan would not pay for rental of a practice room, and she realized that music might not be the most marketable major. Ultimately she earned a B.S., an M.A., and a specialist degree in education, all from the University of Alabama.

I was curious to know what Laura recalled of her own undergraduate teacher education program. She told me that she remembered learning how to write lesson plans and a "devastating" student teaching experience, half of which she completed in Tuscaloosa, the other half in an American school in Mexico City. Neither cooperating teacher gave her guidance, so she resorted to "rummaging through books like the *English Journal* for ways to reach children."

Had she not been committed to teaching, Laura guesses she would have left the profession then, but she had a large loan to repay; according to its terms, half would be waived if she taught for five years.

Laura's first teaching job was in a rural school in Alabama, "back in the days when seventh graders would sit on
your lap and ninth graders would hug you." Faced with the
necessity of teaching herself how to teach, she fell back on
two principles she still believes: "It is my responsibility to
make life easier for my students, and it is possible for me to
make a difference in every child's life."

In the years to follow, Laura earned several graduate
degrees by taking classes at night (and commuting 140 miles)
and during summers. She continued to teach in rural schools
which she recalls with a mixture of good and bad memories.
She described her failure to teach an eleventh grade course
in composition and American literature: "I couldn't figure
out how to integrate the two subdisciplines, so I wound up
teaching a very segmented course and never getting beyond
the Puritan era. I knew I was doing it wrong but I didn't know
how to fix it."

She had a more positive experience several years later,
when she taught a small class of advanced twelfth graders.
She was introduced to the idea of the mini-unit and created
separate folders that students worked on individually. Each
folder was a unit that integrated literature and writing skills.
Seven teachers and one physician emerged from that class,
and Laura still wonders whether her teaching style had
anything to do with that. She tried using a similar method
in later years, but classes had grown too large to handle
effectively, and students had less self-discipline.

A major turning point in Laura's career occurred when
she met a methods professor at the university who encouraged
her to experiment. "She let me create and experiment with
ways of teaching writing. I wasn't having much luck finding
out how to teach children the process. How do you generate
that spark of initiative and make the different skills come
together so that a student has a finished product rather than
separate parts of one? For several years—as an undergraduate,
a graduate, and when I was developing my thesis for my
Specialist degree—this methods professor worked with me.
She allowed me to create what I wanted, to try it, and—if it

worked—to examine why. My own classes became little experimental labs."

In her ninth year of teaching, Laura came to the campus of Central High were, eighteen years later, she still works. Her first few years at Central she taught only advanced composition to twelfth graders and was inundated with student papers. She began to seek workshops that taught management skills as well as techniques for teaching writing.

During the 1970s, as integration swept through the school district, she experienced "culture shock." She had known only one black person in her life and had many misgivings about her ability to understand and communicate with children from backgrounds other than her own. She was sensitive to the need to mitigate her own views and values: "I realized that I could not be a giver of values, but someone who offered options and allowed children to choose among them."

Over the years she also found that her definition of good teaching changed: "At one time I had wanted the children to know everything I knew, because I thought it would make their lives easier. Now I know that they can't know all that I know, so my objective is not to teach them knowledge but how to manipulate knowledge; to love language; and to respect themselves because they can handle it."

I asked her what she was really teaching to students in each of her three courses: advanced composition, regular composition, and American literature. Above all, she said she teaches the students in advanced composition to write varied and sophisticated prose. Despite the complexity of the grammatical structures she teaches them, they are able to use them in their own writing.

She is also teaching her advanced students organizational skills; how to present material in a polished manner; how to incorporate information from many sources without plagiarizing; and how to infer the meanings of new words from their contexts. She pointed out that students in her advanced classes will be able to go to any colleges they desire and that most will become lawyers, physicians, and other kinds of professionals. "They don't need to spend time taking another class or paying a tutor, because I didn't teach them these

skills. There's no limit to what these child
give them the right springboard."

In her regular composition class, Lε
teaching self-discipline, self-respect, basic v
the difference between fact and opinion. S
writing in the context of mundane tasks, like having to send
a parent's note to a teacher explaining why a child was absent
from school. She feels she cannot teach these students the
same reasoning skills as her advanced students, but she
believes those skills will emerge later in their lives:

"I may be wrong; I'm no psychologist. But I firmly believe
that there is a time in every child's life when things click.
There's a time for a child to learn to read, and if he or she
doesn't learn then, it will be harder later on. The advanced
students, whether for environmental or genetic reasons, are
further along developmentally. If I tried to teach the same
things to the kids in my regular class, I would lose them; they
would rebel."

Laura believes that, in part, a teacher's job is to figure
out when a child is ready to learn a particular skill. A test
score is not adequate to indicate this, so Laura said she does
"sneaky things" to find out about each child. For example,
she asks them to write essays in which they talk about their
home lives and leisure activities. She also makes a point of
chatting informally with them between classes. Using these
kinds of information, as well as scores on tests, she decides
to push some students harder than others.

To the students in her American literature classes, Laura
believes she is teaching reading skills, vocabulary, and
cultural relativism. She feels it is important for these students
to be exposed to many different perspectives. For example,
during the course they look at different ways people have
perceived death and an afterlife. She tries to help these
students understand people on their own terms so that they
can interrelate effectively with different kinds of individuals.

She admitted that American literature is probably just
a vehicle for teaching these skills, but insisted that she still
manages to convey something about the beauty of language
or the beauty of the world as it is reflected in language:

hese kids may never go out and read another book by James Fenimore Cooper, but perhaps they will learn something about what they want in a modern hero. They may not read Whitman's *Leaves of Grass*, but they might look more closely at an azalea bloom."

Interestingly, Laura enjoys teaching both ends of the academic spectrum: the brightest as well as the slowest. She spoke of the difficulties involved in teaching basic classes: having to deal with children who are starved for attention and who sometimes direct hostility at her, because they cannot express it to the authorities who really control their lives.

I asked her what she gets from teaching: "These kids make me laugh. They also make me cry, and I get distressed about their problems. They're all basically my children." If she is a good teacher, she said it is because "I have touched some students, made their days better and their lives easier."

Ironically, Laura urged her own son and daughter not to become teachers. "Both are bright and could be anything they wanted. I didn't want them to have the pressures I had—financial, parental, and administrative." Both are grown and out of college now, and Laura remarked that in a two-week period her son earns almost as much as she does in a month.

I asked her if she had any guilt feelings about not wanting her own children to become teachers (i.e., if teachers are so important to society). "Teaching is a vocation," she responded. "There will always be bright, gifted young people who will choose it as a career. I know I am responsible for creating at least ten teachers, some who sacrificed and violated their parents' wishes because they wanted to be like me. So I feel I have given to my profession."

She has worked with at least twenty student teachers over her twenty-eight–year career, and I asked whether she had spotted any trends: "At first they were very good, then mediocre. Now they're either very good or very bad." She speculated that the university may have lowered standards to increase enrollment. This lead to the topic of how to prepare novices for the classroom:

"It takes more than command of one's subject. It takes a special gift to be able to interact with children. But even those with the gift must learn organizational skills. It's a matter of taking a tremendous bulk of material, wading through it until you come up with an organization that's workable for you and for the students. In addition, a teacher must be able to think on the level of the children she teaches. If you can't get to their level, emotionally and academically, you'll never reach them. At the same time, you have to maintain your sense of being an adult." Here Laura mentioned that her husband always tells her that part of her has never grown up.

We ended the interview by talking about the ways children, society, and the job of a teacher have changed over the years. Laura described the "loss of innocence" she has noticed among her students, their lack of self-discipline, and—conversely—the tendency for some to be so competitive that there is the real potential for suicide. She also said that she now has to make a concerted effort to keep in touch with their culture.

She also described the erosion of several academic abilities; today she teaches her regular eleventh graders what she taught to ninth graders twenty years ago. She attributed this to the fact that we are no longer a reading society and that children spend too much time watching TV. "They are so accustomed to having the noise of TV or radio in the background, that they think nothing of speaking when a teacher or classmate is trying to speak."

She attributed their lack of note-taking skills and careless reading to the Xerox machine and the overuse of handouts in classes. She purposely uses few handouts in order to force her students to read and copy material into their notes. It's the only way she can be sure they read it and develop note-taking skills.

Here Laura alluded to Mina Shaughnessy's theory that the written word and the typed word mean different things to a child: "The typed word belongs to someone else, but if a child writes a word, it belongs to him."

As I thanked Laura for giving me so much of her time, I imagined it would be difficult summarizing the interview. She struck me as being a puzzling collection of contradictions: a realist who has led a hard life and has few illusions, but one who also remains extremely flexible and optimistic. In fact, she tells her student teachers that if they are to survive in the classroom, they must come to perceive themselves as balls of silly putty: "When you get thrown against the wall, you just drop down, assume another shape, and get back up."

I sensed she would assume any shape she had to in order to give her students the "springboard" they need. Education and the ability to use language effectively are forms of power to Laura: tools one needs to acquire financial independence and control over one's own life. I wondered if Beth, the professor who teaches the English methods course, shared that belief. I introduce her in the following chapter.

CHAPTER 3

BETH'S COURSE ON METHODS OF TEACHING SECONDARY ENGLISH

I have a feeling that lots of teachers are stuck doing the same things over and over again, because there is no time or money to help them develop new ways. . . I don't blame them, but I think it's boring and that they must be bored doing it.

Beth is completing her first year at the University of Alabama, but she began teaching secondary English methods three years ago in Indiana. At first she patterned her course after her own undergraduate methods course, but over the years she has modified it with insights gained from her graduate studies and her own secondary teaching experiences.

I interviewed her in her office, which was already cluttered with students' portfolios. Beth has a total of eleven years of secondary teaching experience (grades 7–12) in the South, Southwest, and Midwest. She has also taught students with a range of academic abilities and racial/socioeconomic backgrounds. She left the secondary classroom after five years to begin work on a master's degree in English; she returned sporadically while working on a doctorate in English.

Her most recent public school experience was two years ago in Indiana. Although she said she thinks she was a good teacher before pursuing graduate work, her graduate studies made her "light years better. I learned how to fine-tune instruction for kids."

At this point in her career Beth is an established author with literary criticism and anthologies of short stories to her credit. She is currently writing a textbook about how to use portfolios in teaching composition. Her primary reason for leaving secondary teaching was boredom; after the first few years it did not offer her sufficient intellectual stimulation.

Beth needed very little questioning to elicit her beliefs about teaching English. She has a firm grasp of her philosophy and expresses herself forcefully. She speaks with passion, recalling her own secondary teaching experiences with smiles and chuckles.

Beth described her methods course in terms of roughly three components: the teaching of composition, language, and literature. She said she devotes more time to the first two, because she finds that her methods students are least prepared for those areas. She also devotes a few weeks to general professional issues, like instructional planning and organization. Recently she added a brief, one-week field experience to her course, during which students team teach a writing unit to middle school students.

Written assignments for her methods course include three instructional units (for teaching composition, language, and literature, respectively) which are included in a "portfolio" handed in at the end of the semester. The portfolio (usually contained in a letter file) includes a variety of resources for teaching secondary English: notes, stories, lesson plans, activities collected over the semester. She encourages her students to work collaboratively in designing units.

Beth described her course as "theoretically based on a collection of articles that we read and discuss in class." The articles are assembled in a packet that students are required to purchase along with two textbooks: *Teaching Literature in the Secondary School* by Beach and Marshall, and *The English/Language Arts Handbook* by Stephen and Susan Tchudi.

When discussing the teaching of writing, Beth emphasizes the notion of individual processes: "I try to teach my students that there is no such thing as *the* writing process. The traditional cycle most English teachers assume (prewriting,

writing, rewriting) is very reductive. We also talk about different uses of writing and how to evaluate student work. I give my students some of the student writing I have collected over the years, and together we see what we can infer about the students.

There aren't too many tricks or gimmicks for teaching writing, so I try to make my approach fairly theoretical. Teaching composition is such a complicated issue, and few of my methods students have even had one good writing class."

Thus, Beth tries to use articles to introduce her methods students to a "conversation about writing theory." For example, in one article Sondra Perl describes writing processes:

> All the writers I have observed, skilled and unskilled alike, use the process of retrospective structuring while writing. Yet the degree to which they do so varies and seems, in fact, to depend upon the model of the writing process that they have internalized. Those who realize that writing can be a recursive process have an easier time with waiting, looking, and discovering. Those who subscribe to the linear model find themselves easily frustrated when what they write does not immediately correspond to what they planned or when what they produce leaves them with little sense of accomplishment. (Perl, 1980, p. 367)

Authors of other articles allude to a variety of theories: cognitive, rhetorical, even anthropological. The underlying theme of the articles Beth has selected is that an individual's writing process is affected by many variables, including his or her education, the context of the class and school, and what the teacher says about writing. An understanding of that idiosyncratic context should mitigate the teaching of composition.

Beth also has a strong bias about giving kids the freedom to discover things on their own:

"I hate it when a teacher gives students the first sentence of an essay and tells them to finish it. Everything is set up, there's no chance for kids to discover something new. I like to see student-centered instruction, where a teacher tries to contextualize the class around the students and their needs."

I asked Beth how one could teach composition, if writing is such an idiosyncratic process:

"The trick," she said, "is to teach to similarities that cut across idiosyncratic processes. For example, suppose you asked kids to write a profile of someone, and you wanted to help them think of a person to write about. There are activities you could do in class, like free writing, brainstorming, clustering, and looping. Different kids will respond to different methods. Some just sit down and start to write; others would rather prepare a formal outline. I think that what teachers should do is use a variety of methods so they can make every individual writer comfortable in the classroom."

In general Beth does not talk about the specific format for instruction, because she wants her methods students to discover their own styles and attitudes. When her students ask for concrete examples, she purposely provides several, then tries to get them to consider what each option might be saying to pupils about writing:

"For example, you can let students pick their own topics for composition or you can limit them to assigned topics. What's the difference? What message does each communicate?"

Beth does not differentiate the teaching of different written products (essays, research papers, etc.). She said she would like to do so, but does not have time. She relies on the two textbooks to provide students with specific examples. Although she described the texts as being hands-on, she conceded that they do not offer specific lesson plans. For example, *The English/Language Arts Handbook* offers the following concrete advice to preservice teachers:

> — Create time in the class for discussion of ideas and topics proposed by the students: discussion Fridays, for example. Some teachers put a "suggestion box" on their desk as a way for students to propose topics.

> — Be willing to drop what you're doing when students obviously have something powerful and important to talk about.

— Use partnership and small-group work frequently. . .

— Let students choose oral projects along with or instead of written work. This is not to diminish writing, but to appeal to the commonsense observation that many people would rather talk than write. . .
(Tchudi and Tchudi, 1991, pp. 116–17)

Beth defines the teaching of language mechanics (grammar, punctuation, spelling) as the place where the teaching of writing and language overlap. She introduces the teaching of language by discussing what she calls the "big issues." This refers to the politics of language: for example, what it's like to learn in an English class when one is black or Hispanic; what sorts of language an English teacher ought to label as "correct" and "incorrect"; whether teachers should allow kids to write in their native language, if it is other than English.

Beth is adamant about not teaching the mechanics of language as separate skills (grammar, spelling, punctuation, etc.) taken out of an authentic literary context, like reading or writing. In this sense she is a whole language advocate, a notion that her methods students encounter in an article by Ken Goodman:

> Whole language teachers believe that schools exist for kids, not that kids are to be filled and molded by behavior modification or assertive discipline into look-alike, act-alike, talk-alike Barbie and Ken dolls.
>
> Whole language teachers believe there is something special about human learning and human language. They believe all children have language and the ability to learn language, and they reject negative, elitist, racist views of linguistic purity that would limit children to arbitrary "proper" language. Instead, they view their role as helping children to expand on the marvelous language they already use. . .Whole language teachers draw on scientific theories rooted soundly in research from linguistics, language development, sociolinguistics, psycholinguistics, anthropology, and education as they build curriculum, plan instruction, evaluate progress. . .(Goodman, 1986, pp. 25–26)

In discussing children's use of dialect, particularly black dialect, Beth urges her methods students to consider that no dialect is inherently inferior to standard English. On the other hand, children should be told that society associates dialects with particular values. This generally means that if black children want to compete in society beyond their own communities, they must become bilingual.

In general, Beth thinks that grammar is taught badly in schools throughout the country, largely because:

"It is taught by a generation of teachers who were never taught grammar in interesting ways. In the period between 1965 and 1970 (and more recently) much research was conducted about whether teaching grammar actually improved kids' writing. The results said that it didn't. I give those studies to my methods students to read. The only problem with those studies is that they rarely describe the manner in which grammar was taught, which is a key variable. I think grammar needs to be taught inductively, integrated and applied to writing. Teaching stuff about compound/complex sentences and how to punctuate them through the use of worksheets is really terrible."

I asked Beth to give me an illustration of the way she would teach grammar to high school students:

"I might talk about sentence patterns. Maybe I would begin by writing seven sentences on the blackboard that all follow the same grammatical pattern: subject—linking verb—predicate adjective. Then I would write seven different sentences illustrating a different pattern: subject—linking verb—predicate noun.

Then I might say to the pupils: 'Tell me what you see in the first group of sentences. How are they similar?' I'd ask them the same thing about the second group of sentences. Then I'd ask them to compare the two groups: how are they alike and how are they different?

I'd use lots of leading questions to help them realize the common patterns: 'Does the adjective seem to go with any other part of the sentence?' Finally, after prodding them to think and analyze, I'd say: 'Give me a summary sentence that describes the structure of this group of sentences.'

I'd suggest a name for each sentence pattern: 'Let's call this a S-LV-PA (for subject—linking verb—predicate adjective.' But I would point out that people could use different labels for the same structures.

That's how I taught grammar to secondary pupils. I introduced seven different sentence patterns that seemed to work best:

Transitive verbs: subject—verb—object
                subject—verb—indirect object
                subject—verb—direct object—objective
                complement
Linking verbs: subject—linking verb—predicate adjective
                subject—linking verb—predicate noun

Intransitive verb—adverbial modifiers

There—verb—subject ('There is a dog.' 'There' is an expletive).

I'd have kids write sentences in each pattern, and I'd try to make it silly and fun: 'Write me two S-LV-PA or -PN sentences about a famous person in history.' Or I might ask them to find certain sentence patterns in conversation and bring examples back to class."

According to Beth, even the most sophisticated sentence structures can be taught this way. She advises her methods students to avoid using the traditional parts of speech. Instead she talks about "form classes" (noun, verb, adjective, adverb) and "function words" that glue sentences together (conjunctions, determiners, intensifiers). This is the terminology of structural grammar, which she described as more logical and simpler to grasp.

However, Beth does not believe in emphasizing nomenclature or parsing: "Writing grammatical structures is the key. Only by having kids generate structures can you tell whether they understand."

Beth generally dislikes workbooks and traditional grammar texts. Instead she encourages her methods students to take text from literary works and from the writing of pupils themselves: "I believe that teaching language should not be prescriptive, but enriching, stressing that language is full of possibilities. Not that English teachers should apologize for requiring students to master some nomenclature. I just think that grammar is taught in boring ways: the best teaching is by discovery: where a teacher has an agenda but doesn't overtly direct students. Instead she pushes, irritates kids until they arrive at the answers themselves. That's the way I would like to see everything taught in schools."

Everything except spelling and vocabulary, that is, which Beth would not teach at all but would embed in reading and writing activities: "Maybe I'd ask every child to identify five words in a short story that he or she does not know. I hate those state-mandated vocabulary lists that are totally divorced from any context. I might ask kids to keep personal lists of words they misspell in writing assignments, but spelling ability is highly idiosyncratic. Some really smart people can't spell at all. The best thing you can do is teach kids a few rules, a few demon words, and how to use a dictionary. Otherwise you're wasting a lot of time and frustrating them."

When discussing how to evaluate students' written work, Beth tries to disabuse her methods students of the notion of "correctness." Instead of focusing on misspelled words and incorrect punctuation, she suggests that they concentrate on the logic and the thinking that went into a piece of writing.

"Especially in the early drafts, teachers should help writers focus on communicating. Is the writing interesting? Only when they get to the last stage of presenting it, is it appropriate to focus on the mechanics. A grammatically perfect paper that is stupid should never get an A. On the other hand, a smart paper with lots of misspelling should not receive an A either. It's very difficult to evaluate student writing, particularly for my methods students who have read so little of it."

Beth provides her methods students with examples of different grading scales they could use, but refuses to endorse any particular ones. "I tell my students that it's ultimately up to each of them to decide what is important."

When discussing the teaching of literature, Beth stresses the notion of reader response and the need to contextualize a work, making it so real that students are drawn into the world of the text. This means encouraging kids to imagine the historical context of literary works. For example, when introducing *Canterbury Tales* to high school students, a teacher "might begin by asking students what it would be like to live in a world without electricity or telephones."

In teaching literature, Beth again emphasizes using an inductive approach, which she contrasts to the technique she sees most frequently in English classes:

"Teachers have students read a story then answer the questions that follow. Students usually write only at the end of a unit. I'd have them writing every day about something, whether imaginary or about the text. They've got to be writing and thinking about language every day."

Beth also believes that an English teacher should choose literature that is appropriate for the age and ability of pupils. When I asked Beth how one could do this and still follow a mandated curriculum, she explained:

"There may be a curriculum you're supposed to follow, but there are ways to adapt or ignore it. A teacher sometimes has to be subversive, sneaky. If there's a required book that kids can understand, but it's too hard for them to read, I might read it aloud in class. But if a book is totally out of their grasp, I wouldn't teach it. I tell my methods students to use their discretion about following a curriculum. You must make decisions about your class on the basis of what you feel is best for your students. But you also have to cover yourself as a teacher, and so I try to be honest about that as well. A lot depends upon the particular school and curriculum; there's really a continuum of subversion, and I discuss the consequences of subversion and confronting the powers-that-be."

I asked Beth to be more specific about those consequences:

"Like being called on the carpet by your department chairperson. But if kids can't understand a piece of literature, I don't think they should be forced to read it. Just because a curriculum says kids should be ready for a particular book doesn't mean they are."

When she was in the secondary classroom, Beth said she stuck to the curriculum as closely as possible, but never hesitated to enrich or simplify it depending upon her students' needs. "I hate the notion of a body of knowledge that you have to cover. It's the needs of the children that should dictate what you teach."

Beth has had a chance to follow some of her methods students into their student teaching experiences, and I asked her whether they tend to use the concepts she has taught them:

"Some do and some don't. I'd have to give myself a B in that regard. I see many not teaching the way they'd really like to, because they feel coerced by their cooperating teachers. They want to get good grades. I suggest they might ask their cooperating teachers to help them plan and evaluate something new, but most of the student teachers are intimidated. Some cooperating teachers don't want to change their classroom routines; they say it will upset the kids. I don't agree with that at all."

Beth has seen some of her stronger methods students use some of the techniques she suggests when they student teach, but she admitted that many never do, "because they have no imagination and never stop to think: what am I doing? What are the effects? Can I do it a better way? There's a power factor at work, too. So many teachers are afraid of losing control of a class, and they see routines as one way to maintain control."

At the end of the interview, I asked Beth to evaluate the secondary English teaching she has seen in Tuscaloosa. She described it as fairly average and not significantly different from the teaching she has seen in other parts of the country:

"Some teachers are doing good things: some have good intentions. I have a feeling lots of teachers are stuck doing the same things over and over again, because there is no time or money to help them develop new ways. It's hard: it takes reading, thinking, and resources. I don't blame them, but I think it's boring and that they must be bored doing it.

"In general, you see no animation, and that tells kids that the material is boring. If I could give teachers one piece of advice, I would tell them to vary their routines: do something different. Get kids to write more, but don't grade everything they write. One of the best things I ever did was called a 'letter to the teacher.' At the end of a period, I would give my kids ten minutes to write me a letter, telling me about problems they may have been having completing a particular assignment. They were always honest, because they knew the letters wouldn't be graded, and I learned a lot about the kids."

In general, Beth views teaching method as highly personal and urges her methods students to develop their own. However, she also believes that "good methods are inductive and lead to discovery. Bad methods are deductive, where a teacher gets up and lectures for an hour. Unfortunately, many student teachers adopt that pattern, because it's all they've seen in schools and because they fear losing control of a class. Lecture conveys authority."

Beth did concede that a teacher's personality can overcome deficiencies of method. She has seen really fine English teaching that contradicts her biases: "Those English teachers still reached kids, because they were able to motivate them personally by sheer force of personality."

At the end of the interview, I gave Beth a copy of my description of Laura's teaching (exclusive of the description of her cognition). A week later we met again in Beth's office to discuss Laura's practice.

Beth Evaluates My Description
of Laura's Practice

Beth had prepared for the second interview by making notes in the margins of the description. She evaluated Laura's practice by reviewing her notes chronologically. She began by citing several strengths she noticed: namely, the way Laura reviewed prior lessons and previewed the upcoming one; "I admire her cheerfulness and enthusiasm. I think they're the key to her success. I also like her playing the role of advocate, her businesslike tone, and the way she doesn't waste any class time."

Beth then moved to a more general observation: "My overall impression is that there are lots of good things in the

way Laura teaches, as well as a lot of things I wouldn't do—
things that work for her but that wouldn't work for me, that
I'd feel very uncomfortable doing. Sometimes I have the
feeling she's on automatic pilot. To a certain extent. I think
that's necessary when you teach, because there are things
that need to be routinized so you can get the classroom
business over with quickly. But this seems too routinized for
me."

Although Beth then continued to review her notes
chronologically, I have rearranged her evaluation around
seven fundamental arguments that summarize her thoughts:

1. *Beth would define the purpose of learning (to students)
more broadly than did Laura.* Beth noted that Laura told her
advanced composition classes that the purpose of learning
the material was so that students could learn to write well
and be prepared for the advanced placement English exam.
Beth said: "I would talk more generally about how writing
helps students learn and clarify their thinking; how a course
like this would give the students more options as writers.
Laura's approach is too much like teaching to the test; it
emphasizes school. I'd rather emphasize learning for the sake
of good writing and the intellectual activity that goes with
it. I suspect that Laura's class was driven by the need to cover
material rather than by the students' needs or desires."

2. *The parts-to-whole approach to teaching writing (that
Laura uses) does not work.* Beth was critical of Laura's rather
segmented way of teaching composition through grammar:
"I don't object to teaching grammar, but at this point it ought
to be dealt with as a review only. I don't think grammar
should be embedded in a composition course, because research
indicates that way of teaching writing doesn't work: that is,
building separate skills. You have to get students writing
whole compositions from the very beginning, then address
problems in their writing as they occur naturally."

Here I questioned whether Beth based this opinion on
research only or whether it was also validated by her own
experiences in secondary classrooms:

"I've tried the parts-to-whole approach and I got much
better results the other way: by starting and continuing to
focus on students' writing."

At this point I asked whether the secondary students Beth taught resembled Laura's. Beth answered that the students in Laura's regular composition class were most similar to students she had known.

3. *Laura's explanations of grammar were often more complicated and confusing than they need be.* In general, Beth felt that Laura made grammar more difficult than necessary. Beth cited the following examples: Laura's distinction between finite and nonfinite verbals ("She's losing sight of the bigger picture; this is finer than it need be"); Laura's definition of a gerund ("Why not just say that a gerund has the form of a verb and the function of a noun?"); the way Laura combined two short sentences to illustrate the creation of nominative absolutes ("She makes it sound harder than it is; it's just a sentence with the auxiliary verb collapsed out").

4. *The process of composing sentences, as presented by Laura, does not match descriptions of how writers really write.* Beth thought that Laura's device of having her students write original sentences patterned after those of famous authors was a legitimate technique. However, she questioned the process of composing the original sentences: "You don't start with the predicate verb, you start with the subject. Laura's way doesn't even seem cognitively correct. I've spent lots of time researching how authors really write, and Laura's way doesn't resemble anything I've ever read." Beth alluded to a similar point when discussing the steps Laura indicated were involved in writing a periodic sentence: "It doesn't work that way in real life. You're always dealing with a particular content, and it's the content that determines how you structure sentences."

5. *Beth prefers inductive techniques that require students to infer rules.* The aspects of Laura's lessons with which Beth was most uncomfortable were the use of "study sheets" (with grammatical rules and examples) and the dictating of grammatical rules into students' notes. "I don't like rules," she admitted frankly. "I like to think of them as generalizations rather than rules, and I want students to infer them and put them in their own words. The fact that Laura has

to keep reminding students of the rules tells me that they haven't sunk in."

Here I asked: What if it took a teacher three times longer to draw generalizations out of the students? Wouldn't the process become frustrating and boring? Beth responded:

"The trick is to lead students to inferences, to push and prod them. I wouldn't let it go on so long that it became boring. Laura's way is too lazy for kids. They don't have to do anything; she gives them all the answers and all they have to do is memorize them."

6. *Beth would spend more time having students write grammatical structures rather than identifying and parsing them.* Beth identified several points in Laura's lessons where she (Beth) would require students to generate more original text. One was the exercise where Laura asked students to combine several short sentences into one long sentence incorporating an absolute. Beth described the way she would handle this:

"I might start with two sentences and say, 'How could we combine these into one sentence?' I'd get the students to tell me several ways. If they didn't come up with an absolute construction, I'd suggest it. Then I'd write it on the board and ask them how they liked it: 'What did I do to make that sentence?' They'd tell me and we'd practice a few more together. At that point I'd give them a list of base clauses and ask *them* to come up with the modifying ideas which they would incorporate into absolutes. I wouldn't give them the modifying elements."

Beth made a similar point about teaching punctuation: "This is so boring. Why not take some sentences from the students' own writing, put them on a transparency and ask the students to tell her where to place punctuation marks. Then ask the students to come up with the rules. I'd also put students into small groups and have them write sentences collaboratively."

7. *When teaching language, Beth would not emphasize correctness, but various options.* Beth noted that Laura seemed to emphasize correctness in her composition classes. I

reminded Beth that her students faced an advanced placement exam. How could she avoid addressing correctness?

To this Beth responded: "I'd say, 'Here's how it works. In certain situations, like tests, you have to be correct and assume that you're writing for a super-standard, formal audience. But that's not how we usually use language.'"

"Are you suggesting that Laura is too much of a purist for you?" I asked.

"Exactly," said Beth. "I'm not sure she wants her students to know *why* we make the language choices we do and the implications of those choices. To me, that's everything."

To illustrate what she meant, Beth gave two examples. One was Laura's teaching of the periodic versus loose sentence. "I would like to see her talk about the psychological effect of each kind of sentence on the reader. What kinds of thinking does each type of sentence force, in both readers and writers? Why do we usually write loose rather than periodic sentences? Because they're easier; periodic sentences are hard; you have to think back."

The second example concerned Laura's general approach to grammar: "I would tell students the history of grammar. We borrowed it from the Latin in the eighteenth century, and that's why we have so many stupid rules: some rules that fit Latin just don't fit English. A teacher ought to explain that to students, also that they are 'conventions' more than logical rules, which is why many don't work and are dying out. We are required to continue using pure, formal English on special occasions, like taking AP tests."

The final section of Beth's commentary concerned Laura's instruction in the American literature classes: "It doesn't sound like the students are being engaged. I know how difficult it is when you are working with students who are deficient in reading skills, but sometimes teachers give up on them—don't give them credit for having any imagination."

I reminded Beth that my description of Laura's classes captured only a small part of her practice and that she (Laura) probably used a wider variety of media and formats than my description suggested. I also asked Beth if she could suggest specific ways a teacher might engage these students.

"I'd try more imaginative tasks," she responded. "I like the way Laura compared the life of a Puritan woman with that of a modern woman. I'd like to see her pursue that, perhaps as a writing assignment or group work. I would like to see students forced to draw more on their own experiences and to connect them to literature."

She made similar points about Laura's lesson on Romanticism: "I'd never start a unit like this. Instead I'd talk about the artificiality of titles, like 'Romanticism,' or 'Classicism.' Instead of using labels, I'd explain to the students that during this period of time many writers seemed to be doing similar things. After the unit, after we had read different authors, I would summarize and ask the students to infer the common themes we had found among the authors."

There were several points in Laura's lessons that Beth pointed out as natural bridges to students' own lives. One was the notion of a pen name: "Why not ask students to pick pen names. Write them on the board and see if the class could guess which name belonged to which students."

When Beth had completed critiquing my description of Laura's practice, I asked her to pretend that I were one of her methods students: "I've just taken your course and then observed Laura. Could you explain to me how Laura can be a good teacher but not use any of the methods you taught me in your methods course?"

Beth thought for several minutes before answering: "Well, I'd say that she's a good teacher but that she could be an even better teacher. Basically she's good, because she's figured out how to motivate her students."

"Does that end justify any method?" I asked.

"That's a difficult question," Beth answered. "Some methods are preferable, but perhaps the end does justify the means sometimes."

I tried to get at the issue another way: why did Beth think so many experienced teachers did *not* use inductive methods?

"Sometimes teachers are tired. Sometimes they don't give kids credit for any imagination. Some teachers might be afraid of inductive methods because they're messy. You can't be sure what kids put in their class notes, but if you dictate the notes you cover yourself. Sometimes kids get excited during inductive lessons, and a teacher might feel that he or she is losing control. The principal might pass the classroom, hear noise, and assume teaching is not occurring. I know there are many good reasons teachers may want to keep a lid on the energy of kids."

Suppose teachers learned about inductive methods—that they were not as dangerous as they may seem—did Beth think teachers would rush out and start using them?

"No. In some cases they may be incompatible with a teacher's personality. I tell my methods students to experiment with different methods, to find out which are most comfortable for them."

"You mean, you wouldn't mind if they decided to lecture to kids?" I asked.

"I wouldn't necessarily object," Beth said. "It would depend on the kind of lecture and whether other methods were also used. One has to mitigate the teacher's comfort with the needs of the students. I just think of my own classroom experience: when I took risks, sometimes the most wonderful things happened. That's why I think teachers need to open up and let things happen."

I posed a final question: Did Beth think that Laura's objectives as an English teacher were the same as her own when she was teaching secondary students? When Beth indicated, yes, I asked her to state them:

"To help young people be more judicious and knowledgeable in their use of language, both in reading and writing."

I found that very interesting, because, in fact, I was not at all certain that Laura would agree with that statement. I was eager to find out how she would react to the rest of Beth's pedagogical philosophy. I gave Laura a copy of this chapter and scheduled an interview with her for one week later. A description of that interview and Laura's responses to Beth appear in the following chapter.

CHAPTER 4

LAURA'S RESPONSE TO BETH

Telling preservice teachers that they should use their discretion about following the curriculum seems irresponsible, in that it may be giving novices an unrealistic picture of their professional power.

I met Laura in her classroom after school to interview her about her response to Beth's chapter. She surprised me with an eight-page (typed single-space) essay. She explained that she had not fully realized the significance of this project until she had read Beth's views: "After my first reading, I decided that I needed not only to reread the material several times, but also to spend some time searching my own philosophy so that I could justify what I had always taken for granted. I did not want to make rash judgments, particularly in view of the vast differences between our perspectives (mine and Beth's)."

In her essay Laura responded to Beth's views as they appeared chronologically in chapter 3. I reorganized the essay around the two points that appeared to underlie Laura's concerns: questions about the appropriateness of (a) advice Beth gives to her methods students, and (b) the activities and beliefs Beth endorses for teaching secondary students. With the exception of that reorganization and some minor editing, what follows is Laura's own words:

Evaluating the Advice Beth Gives
to Methods Students

Although Beth recognizes the cultural differences among children in an English class, she seems to assume that a teacher can adhere to a single theory of teaching. I see that as contradictory. Because of the diversity of the children I teach, I have to adopt and adapt some of whatever methods I encounter. I would want preservice teachers to understand that they can never limit themselves, lest they limit their students.

I commend Beth on wanting her methods students to discover their own styles and attitudes. However, I question whether this is a feasible expectation at their point of professional development. She herself admits that "few. . . have even had one good writing class" when they come to her. On what information can they make sound decisions about personal teaching styles?

I am frankly frightened by her advising her methods students to defy (albeit subtly) curriculum guides that teachers and administrators have decided are in the best interests of students. Telling preservice teachers that they should "use their discretion about following the curriculum" seems irresponsible, in that it may be giving novices an unrealistic picture of their professional power. For a beginning teacher, that sort of attitude can result in transfer or even dismissal.

Taking it upon oneself to alter the curriculum could cause serious problems for students. Next year's teachers will expect students to know what was designated in this year's curriculum; if the content isn't taught, it is the student who will suffer. If a teacher feels that there is a serious problem with the curriculum for the majority of students, she has valid avenues for initiating change, and I would advise her working through those options rather than trying to be "sneaky" (Beth's word). In the school systems where I have taught, much time and study are invested in writing curriculum guides; encouraging beginning teachers to disregard these seems unwise.

I can understand how Beth, as a teacher of composition and language, hates the notion of "body of knowledge that you have to cover." However, Beth herself accepts this reality in that she prepares a body of knowledge that she expects her methods students to cover. It is a reality of any class or course, and suggesting to preservice teachers that it isn't would be misleading.

In the Curriculum Guide issued by the Alabama State Department of Education, the state has dictated a "body of knowledge" for each grade and subject. If every teacher modified it, continuity would be destroyed; it is doubtful whether high school students would obtain the competencies they need in order to graduate.

Similarly, I question the attitude that Beth implies when she refers to the many "stupid rules" of English usage and says that "formal English" is important on "special occasions" only, like taking AP exams. Isn't that attitude a bit narrow? Shouldn't Beth's methods students be given the opportunity to make such decisions on their own? The observation that formal (correct) English is appropriate only for special occasions seems too restrictive. Have colleges and the business world really become so relaxed about the use of correct English? Again, I wonder if she is misleading her methods students.

Beth alludes to pressures from policies and other constraints, but she seems to pass these off as relatively minor obstacles for teachers to overcome. There are very real expectations for performance that teachers must acknowledge: expectations of administrators and state departments of education, students and parents, colleges and the business world. By denying the importance of meeting those expectations, Beth may be giving her methods students an unrealistic picture of what a teaching career will demand of them.

Beth advises her students that the best way to address students' mechanical (language) problems is in student writing, "as they occur naturally." Here I question Beth's understanding of the wide diversity in language skills that can exist in a class of thirty-five high school students. If new teachers are to be prepared to handle heterogeneous classes, they may have to acquire a more direct approach to teaching the mechanics of language. Fashioning a separate curriculum for each student's unique needs (the logical outcome of Beth's approach) leads to an incoherent, highly segmented class and a frustrated, overworked teacher.

I liked Beth's reference to the teacher's personality and her suggestion that her students try a variety of methods until they find what is best suited to them. However, I do not believe that a successful teacher can follow only one method. Quite the contrary, a good teacher is one able to give students what they need and willing to employ any method that may be required.

A good teacher helps students investigate what they want from life and then helps them find paths to those objectives. Like Robert Frost, students should be allowed to stand where "two roads diverge," and it is a teacher's job to take students to that fork in the road without biasing them in either direction.

Finally, I want to respond to Beth's statement that her methods students "have no imagination and never stop to question." Preservice candidates who have no imagination and who are unable or unwilling to question do not belong in the classroom. To encourage them to continue in a preservice program may be dooming them to failure in their student teaching experiences. On a larger level, it perpetuates mediocrity.

Evaluating Practices that Beth Endorses for Teaching Secondary Students

First I want to note that Beth seems to have some misconceptions about the practices of most English teachers. Her suggestion that most teachers assign writing only at the end of a unit or in response to questions at the end of a story is a great overgeneralization. The majority of teachers with whom I have worked rarely, if ever, conform to that portrait.

By the same token, I must take issue with Beth's contention that students should write something every day. An English teacher typically has over 100 students. It is unrealistic to expect a teacher to respond to 100 assignments every day. Even if she does not grade them, the time needed to read through them is prohibitive. Teachers also have lesson plans to prepare, families for whom to care, and many other responsibilities.

In general I question to what degree Beth is in touch with today's secondary students. I have taught English and music to students from grades 7 through the sophomore year in college. Interestingly, I have found that, regardless of age, students hold the same expectations for teachers, expectations which are at variance with those expressed by Beth.

I question Beth's suggestion about avoiding the traditional terminology of grammar. Why give children a new terminology that does not correspond with their texts or past experiences? Beth says she dislikes workbooks and traditional grammar texts. So do I, but I acknowledge that using them gives some students great comfort and confidence. One can always supplement texts, as I do, with prose taken from literary works.

Similarly, Beth said that she doesn't like rules of English usage. Beth and I may not like rules, but students do. They often ask for specific rules, because they feel comfortable having something on which to lean. Why deny them this security? I do not hesitate to give a rule when asked, nor do I hesitate (when it is appropriate) to force students to generate their own rules through inductive reasoning.

Some of the activities Beth suggested seem particularly inappropriate for secondary students. For example, she suggests asking students to write the teacher a letter at the end of the period. How frequently is this to occur? As a daily exercise, it would ultimately consume one-fifth of the semester—a proportion of instructional time I would find hard to justify when there are so many important objectives to address.

I was somewhat amused by Beth's suggestion about asking students to invent their own pen names. First, I question spending class time on such an activity for high school juniors. Second, my students know all about "pen names." Several have pen names stitched across the backs of their jackets to connect them with particular social groups. Introducing a discussion about personal pen names would only give students an opportunity to allude to suggestive or obscene names. Why give them the chance to focus on the negative as opposed to the academic?

I found Beth's suggestions about teaching sentence structure interesting and, in fact, they are equivalent to the format I use for review. However, I have found that format to be ineffective for introducing new material, especially in that it confuses weaker students. Having access to diverse methods is critical when it comes to introducing new material. If I always presented material in the same way, students would become apathetic.

I have a similar concern about Beth's suggestion that students be forced to generate their own sentences containing particular structures. Beth assumes that students possess enough knowledge about sophisticated grammatical structures (absolutes) to generate them independently, without guided practice in combining sentences. I often use the approach she suggested, but not when material is relatively new.

Forcing students to generate their own sentences independently, without first building a solid foundation of knowledge, will ultimately make it more difficult for them to grasp relationships. It also sets them up for failure rather than success, primarily because the inexperienced writer must make so many errors before creating the structure in question. I prefer to start off with simpler, less stressful tasks that are more likely to reinforce them positively.

I do not stop at sentence structure, as Beth implies. Once students have grasped a concept and a particular grammatical structure, we discuss how that type of sentence is most effectively used within a paragraph. Dona did not happen to observe that aspect of my composition course. The concept of building paragraphs and essays from varied, complex stylistic sentences is a major objective of twelfth-grade composition classes. So my goal becomes the preparation of the sentence itself, with an introduction of its purpose. The manipulation of the sentence can be taught later.

On a more general level I am concerned that Beth does not believe in teaching spelling and vocabulary directly (as separate skills). Regardless of the "whole language" philosophy, how can she justify *not* teaching them to students who must demonstrate competency on college entrance exams?

In general I agree with Beth about the importance of teaching composition skills along with logical thinking and self-expression. However, I wonder if she has tried to teach this way to students who do not write in whole sentences. Before students can be logical or interesting in their writing, they need to be coherent. So many English teachers focus on the interest level of writing, rather than the mechanics, that many high school students are unable to meet the demands of the workplace. Students need a sound vocabulary (oral and written) whether they are bound for college or the work force. How can this be ignored?

A related issue concerns Beth's belief that grammar should be taught in conjunction with composition *only as review*. It is difficult to teach concepts in review, when students have not yet mastered them. The state requires that I teach grammar in conjunction with composition. More importantly, students who expect to enter college must know how to handle grammatical aspects of their language. In 1989 college entrance tests began to place even greater emphasis on grammatical knowledge; 53 percent of the English test on the Enhanced ACT is specifically usage/mechanics. Were I merely to review rather than teach grammar, I would be cheating my advanced composition students.

This leads me to the more general issue of motivating students with grades and "teaching to the test." Beth said that my classes seemed to be "driven by the need to cover material rather than by the students' needs or desires." I do not see the two as contradictory. Students' needs overlap their desires. They need and want to do well in their twelfth-grade composition class and on their college entrance exams.

The scores students obtain on their AP exams and the levels of competency they exhibit in writing applications for college will determine scholarships as well as admission. For some of these children, no scholarship means no college. For others, the AP credit means money not granted through scholarships. As a teacher, I have no right to deny them that educaitonal opportunity by ignoring the importance of grades and tests.

I get continuous feedback from twelfth-grade teachers indicating that my students excel as leaders in written and oral activities. Students and their parents have thanked me for jumps of five to seven points on the language section of the ACT, after the students have taken my composition course. With such specific evidence of success, I cannot accept the observation that it is wrong to teach to the test.

Beth says that teachers should emphasize learning for its own sake rather than for grades. However, I noted that *her* students appear to be as concerned about grades as are mine (I refer to Beth's comments about student teachers being concerned about getting good grades). Is there a contradiction here? Is there not within each of us an inherent need to have a concrete, albeit symbolic, evaluation of our performance on a particular task? If so, then we cannot deny giving or referring to grades as a motivation in the classroom.

The question of motivation impelled me to conduct a survey in each of my classes. I asked students to answer two questions anonymously. First, I asked them to list in order of importance the three things they had wanted to get from their English class this year. Then I asked them to indicate which they had received thus far; they were free to indicate that they had received something other than what they had expected. I told my students that I planned to use their responses to redirect course objectives for the remainder of the year and to evaluate my own teaching. Since I ask students to evaluate my classes at the end of each semester, conducting a survey did not seem unusual.

With Dona's help, I computed the percentages of responses per category for the first question (Table 4.1). Grades emerged as the most important objective, ranging from 22 percent of

Table 4.1
Survey of Laura's Classes
Responses to: List in Order of Importance Three Things You Expected to Get out of This Class

Grades

	1	2	3	4	5
First	41	22	56	64	77
Second	18	11	4	29	8
Third	-	28	11	-	-

Preparation for College/Tests/Next Year

	1	2	3	4	5
First	-	6	7	7	-
Second	6	11	11	14	-
Third	18	17	-	-	-

Literature Skills

	1	2	3	4	5
First	6	17	-	-	-
Second	24	33	-	-	-
Third	12	6	-	-	-

Days Off

	1	2	3	4	5
First	-	-	36	-	-
Second	-	-	-	-	-
Third	-	-	-	-	-

Knowledge

	1	2	3	4	5
First	-	-	33	14	15
Second	-	-	26	7	31
Third	-	-	15	36	15

Writing Skills

	1	2	3	4	5
First	47	44	-	-	-
Second	18	28	-	-	-
Third	12	17	-	-	-

A Good Teacher

	1	2	3	4	5
First	-	-	-	14	-
Second	-	-	-	-	-
Third	-	-	11	-	-

New Ideas

	1	2	3	4	5
First	-	-	-	-	-
Second	-	-	-	-	-
Third	-	-	6	-	-

No Homework

	1	2	3	4	5
First	-	-	-	-	-
Second	-	-	-	11	-
Third	-	-	-	-	-

Understanding of Language/New Vocabulary

	1	2	3	4	5
First	12	6	-	-	-
Second	6	6	-	-	-
Third	6	-	-	-	-

Friends

	1	2	3	4	5
First	-	-	-	-	-
Second	-	-	-	11	-
Third	-	-	-	-	-

Note: Results are listed for Laura's five classes in the following order: advanced composition, advanced composition, regular composition, American literature, American literature. The numbers represent the percentages of total students who were in attendance in each class the day the survey was taken: 17, 18, 27, 14, 13. The relatively low attendance was due to the scheduling of a field trip.

Table 4.2
Survey of Laura's Classes
Responses to: What Have You Received from This Class Thus Far?

	Advanced composition (n = 17)	Advanced composition (n = 18)	Regular composition (n = 27)	American literature (n = 14)	American literature (n = 13)
Grades	29	6	37	29	39
Improvement in writing skills	47	44	-	21	-
Knowledge/new ideas	-	6	19	43	23
Preparation for college/test/ next year	-	17	-	14	-
A good teacher	-	-	15	7	-
Respect for others	6	-	-	-	-

Note: Numbers entered in this table represent the percentages of total students who were in attendance in each class the day the survey was taken. The relatively low attendance was due to the scheduling of a field trip.

responses in one of the advanced composition classes to 77 percent in one of the American literature classes. The variety of responses to this question was also interesting: writing and literature skills; a good teacher; preparation for college/tests/next year; no homework; friends; days off (!).

Responses to the second question about what students felt they had received (Table 4.2) indicated that the students in advanced composition felt they had improved their writing and literature skills. Those in American literature felt they had acquired new knowledge and the grades they had expected.

Thus, as noble as Beth's contention sounds, it does not appear to reflect the needs and desires of the students themselves. I have found that even advanced students find little challenge in the acquisition of knowledge for its own sake. Thirty-six percent of the students in one American literature class has as their priority getting "day off with no work." Are these the students Beth expects to motivate by emphasizing "learning for the sake of good writing and the intellectual activity that goes with it"?

Concluding Observations

Beth and I were asked to evaluate each other on the basis of a highly restricted view of practice. As a result both of us undoubtedly drew some incorrect conclusions. However, this experience is equivalent to the way inservice teachers are evaluated by administrators and the way student teachers are evaluated by university supervisors. All of a teacher's skills and potential are judged by one thirty- to fifty-minute observation. How can we pretend such evaluations are valid?

I was impressed by how differently Beth and I view the same terrain. How could that happen? Beth has not been so long out of the classroom that she would have forgotten the realities. Perhaps a clue can be found in Beth's admission that she left the secondary classroom because it did not offer sufficient intellectual stimulation.

That comment amazed me, for I cannot recall ever having a boring day as a teacher. I cannot comprehend how the challenge of meeting students' needs could fail to be intellectually stimulating. Beth and I must be very different sorts of individuals. Perhaps that accounts for the polar distance between our beliefs.

Dona concluded Beth's chapter wondering if I would agree with Beth's definition of the objectives of an English teacher: "To help young people be more judicious and knowledgeable in their use of language, both in reading and writing." In fact, I do not agree, because it is much too narrow.

Language and literature are merely tools that students can use to chart their own paths in life. And, like Frost, for each student any road becomes "the one less traveled," and he or she needs equipment that can make the uncharted journey easier. As an English teacher, I feel I am responsible for giving students sound and ready tools to make their lives—their roads—a little easier.

CHAPTER 5

WHAT I SAW
IN JIM'S CLASSROOM

I don't feel intrinsically superior to any of my students; some are probably smarter than me and as adults will earn more money than me. I have no desire to wield power or to make their lives difficult. I respect them and want to help them acquire the basic knowledge of American history that they are expected to have.

In the spring semester of 1992, Jim's schedule included two preparations: eleventh-grade American history (two advanced placement classes, one regular class) and an elective course in world history (one class, mostly seniors). The only criterion for enrollment in the advanced placement (AP) classes is that students meet state guidelines for earning an Advanced Academic (rather than a Standard Academic) Diploma. Those two terms generally distinguish college-bound and vocational students.

Jim has a commanding presence in the classroom, attributable to his size (a solid six feet) and his rich baritone voice. However, there is nothing formal or intimidating about his classes. Quite the contrary. Because he sells candy to help raise money for the junior/senior prom, there is usually a crowd of students at the front of the room between periods to make purchases. Jim allows his students to eat snacks and soft drinks in his classroom. The rate at which some students in his first two periods consumed snacks suggested this was their first food of the day. It is interesting to note that Jim's classroom is immaculate; one will not find empty wrappers or soft drink cans on the floor or on the desks.

Jim's primary instructional format is narrative. He calls it lecture, but storytelling would be a more accurate term. Perched on the edge of a student's desk or pacing back and forth in front of the room, Jim spins personal, episodic tales of exotic times and places. Like any good storyteller, he never begins without reviewing the prior episode and forecasting the episode to come.

His monologues are entertaining, at times mesmerizing, largely because of his highly articulate delivery. During the twelve hours I sat in his classroom, I never once heard him stumble or grope for a word. He is in complete control of the forces of time and history. As I watched students listen and take notes, I sensed that they derived great security from this approach.

Jim insists that there is nothing special about the way he presents the content of his courses; that if he is regarded as an effective teacher, it is because of his personality and easy rapport with students. His affection for them is obvious, as he drapes his arm across a student's shoulder and jokes.

Like Laura, Jim gives students a firm foundation of information which they are ultimately asked to recall, explain, or—in the case of his AP students—use to answer difficult essays. Also like Laura, Jim takes full responsibility for dictating class notes; it is his organization, perspective, and values that count. Although his American history classes have textbooks, class notes take priority. Only at the end of a unit does Jim integrate selected material from the text.

Students in his world history class are even more dependent on class notes, because they have no textbooks. Funding makes it difficult for administrators to justify purchasing a set of expensive books for a one-semester elective that is sometimes cancelled for lack of enrollment.

Each lesson I observed consisted of a brisk, concentrated narrative that ran thirty-five to forty-five minutes in length. I found the task of taking notes very challenging. Although Jim told me that he covers material more slowly in his regular classes than in his AP classes, I noticed no significant difference in pace. However, students in his regular classes often asked him to repeat important points.

I could identify two ways in which Jim adapted his style for less academically able students. First, he provided them with written outlines of the class notes, listing key words and phrases and enough space for students to enter their own notes. The second adaptation concerned the nature of tests and written assignments. Students in the AP classes were required to write essays in which they interrelated facts, argued, and justified generalizations. Students in the regular classes took short-answer tests and answered questions listed at the end of textbook chapters. These questions usually asked them to locate particular information within the chapter and explain it in their own words.

The motivation to master content in all of Jim's classes is to do well on tests and get good grades. For the AP students there is the additional incentive of preparing for the advanced placement college entrance exam in American history. Jim positions himself as a valuable ally in the achievement of both goals. For example, in talking with students in the regular American history class about the grading period about to end, Jim remarked:

> We've got seven grades for you now, all on a twenty-point scale. That scale seems to be working to your advantage; most of you have done well. If we take a quiz today, we'll have eight grades. Which would you prefer next week: another twenty-point test or a major exam?

Similarly, Jim explained to his AP students the rationale behind a series of essays he was assigning for homework:

> For those of you who will be taking the AP test in American history, you need to become familiar with something called a "document-based question." It's sort of a glorified essay that presents you with excerpts from historical documents, asks you to take a position on a question regarding them, and to defend your position. I want to give you some exposure to it, so you won't be surprised when you see it

on the AP exam. There's usually one question on American foreign policy, and the group of essays listed on your assignment sheet will give you the foundation you need to handle the document-based question on foreign policy should one appear. Let's look at it together.

[Jim reads the essay question as follows] "Early U. S. foreign policy was primarily a defensive reaction to perceived or actual threats from Europe. Assess the validity of this generalization with reference to U.S. foreign policy on two major issues during the period 1789–1825."

Notice the phrase, "assess the validity of this generalization." That phrase has appeared on every AP test I've seen. It means you must take a stand and defend it with supporting evidence. To answer this question, you could look at early presidents, decide whether their foreign policy was defensive or aggressive, and give specific examples.

Because his monologues are so concentrated, Jim seems to make a point of not filling the whole sixty-minute period. Instead he appears to arrange purposely for some "down time" at the end of the period. He often uses this time to look at the rough drafts of essay assignments or to discuss upcoming school events of interest. The AP classes I observed were relatively small (about twenty students, 25 percent of whom were black) compared to the regular classes (twenty-five students, 40–60 percent black). Jim later explained that enrollments in all classes were always much higher in the fall semester.

For the most part, Jim interacts with students as a whole class. However, he occasionally has students work in small groups to check homework. During the hours I observed Jim's classes I saw no disciplinary problems. Jim was always in total control, even when shifting from the freewheeling humor of an informal chat to a serious discussion of an upcoming test. I was particularly intrigued by Jim's ability to sense when individual students were having difficulty following his monologue. Occasionally he would pause to ask a particular student: "What's wrong, Ray? Have I lost you?"

When I viewed Jim's narratives analytically, I was able to identify three devices he uses to build bridges from the alien past to the familiar present. Sometimes he stressed the human psychology underlying historical events, asking his students to imagine themselves in similar situations. For example, when explaining how President Grant's loyalty implicated him in his friends' illegal activities, Jim remarked: "Some of you might get yourselves into sticky situations someday, because you are loyal to your friends."

A second device Jim used was relating content to students' personal experiences: "Have any of you ever visited an Indian reservation? Robert, you did? [Robert explains he visited two: one in North Carolina, the other in New Mexico.] Which one looked more prosperous? [Robert indicates the one in North Carolina.] That's because the reservations on the East Coast are really tourist traps and give a false impression of Indian life-style. The reservations in the Southwest display the true poverty and bleakness of Indian life."

A variant of this technique involved comparing the past to something in current events. For example, Jim attempted to define a "protectorate" in terms of the U.S. presence in Kuwait after the Gulf War: "If Kuwait were our protectorate, we'd be telling them how much to charge for their oil and when to sit down and negotiate with Israel. But we don't have those powers; we're just there to help them rebuild."

Occasionally explaining the past in terms of something familiar to students involved the use of analogies. The following verbatim excerpt taken from Jim's regular American history class illustrates this technique. Jim was trying to explain how the American businessman of the late nineteenth century was instrumental in forcing the United States out of its isolationism:

> **Jim:** The third factor that helped the U.S. break out of its isolationist attitude was the American businessman. It's pretty simple, really. If you were a businessman going into business in Tuscaloosa, you'd compete with similar businesses in surrounding cities. If you had a larger business, you would compete with businessmen in other states,

maybe even other countries. At this point in history American businessmen were at a disadvantage, because the U.S. had not passed enough laws that gave them an edge in national markets. Now they want the government to start writing some laws like that.

Student: What do you mean by, "compete"?

Jim: Well, let's say there is a company in the U.S. that is producing T-shirts, and there's another company in France. The market for T-shirts is in China; they sell millions of T-shirts there. The French government has given French businessmen an edge; it has passed laws that allow the French businessmen to sell shirts in China at a low price. But there are no American laws that do this for the American businessmen; they get no break in cargo rates, taxes, etc.

The third device Jim used to help translate the past was relating it to his own experiences, especially when he was in military service. This technique is illustrated in the excerpt that follows. Jim was explaining an event that contributed to the Chilean Crisis in the 1880s. Like most of his monologues, it is couched in the present and future tenses:

> Let's start with the Chilean Crisis. Here we are dealing with a scenario that repeats itself in Latin America many times in the future. Instead of replacing one political leader with another through an election, there is a guerrilla uprising. The U.S. government believed that the Chilean government in power was worth retaining, so we try to frustrate the guerrillas. One thing the U.S. does is to establish a blockade along the coast to stop arms from reaching the guerrillas.
>
> (By the way, the U.S. used the same strategy with Cuba in the 1960s.)
>
> In the case of Chile, we are not successful in stopping the guerrillas. They do manage to overthrow the government, and once the guerrillas are in power they are not at all friendly to the U.S.

This is followed by a second, accidental event off the Chilean coast, where the U.S. happens to have a ship called the *Baltimore*. The captain of the *Baltimore* thinks some of his crew need some shore time, so he lets them go into a small Chilean town, and a riot erupts in which several American sailors are killed.

The U.S. president at that time, Harrison, is very upset about this and places certain demands on Chile. First, he wants an apology. Now, while an apology from an individual isn't hard to get (Kelly over there apologizes every time he leaves the room), an apology from a country can be very difficult to obtain.

Harrison's second condition is that Chile has to make an indemnity payment. To be crude about it, the U.S. sets a price on human life and demands payment for the sailors that were killed. Now, those of you who take chemistry from Mrs. A. probably learned that the human body is worth about twelve to fourteen dollars in chemicals. That's not the kind of worth we're talking about here.

The U.S. is demanding reimbursement for the training that they invested in the sailors. Those who were officers are considered more valuable than those who were enlisted men. Let me give you a specific example of how they go about figuring this. When I graduated from college and went into the military, I went through nine to eleven weeks of Ranger schooling. At the end of the school, we were told that the value of the training was one million dollars per officer. That's a lot of money for the government to invest in a group of officers. Now maybe you can see why the government figured that if naval officers were killed, they were worth more than the enlisted men and justified an indemnity payment.

The only way to convey the entertaining nature of Jim's episodes of history is to present an entire monologue. The one I have chosen is from his world history class. I had to struggle to record it verbatim:

Before we begin our notes for today, let's do a little reviewing. Yesterday we were talking about Queen Anne, the last of the Stuart line. The Parliament knows that when she dies, there will not be a Stuart heir, so they sign the Act of Settlement that helped them identify her nearest Protestant relative. In 1714, when Anne dies, Parliament invites a new family, the Hanovers (who were German), to England, and George I comes to the English throne.

Today we're going to look at two things: the growing power of Parliament and the growing power of the Whigs over the Tories. Let's look at the Parliament first.

There are several indications that the power of Parliament is growing. First, for the second time, it picks the person who will inherit the English throne. Second, Parliament is gaining greater control over the economy. In 1694 it created the Bank of England. Then in 1707 the Act of Union is passed, which legally joins England and Scotland and creates Great Britain. Unification immediately opens more markets and improves the economy, and Parliament gets to write all the laws for the new union.

You can see the benefits of unification today in Germany. Have you been watching the Winter Olympics on TV? Who's winning most of the gold medals? [Students call out, Germany.] Yes. Germany. Do you know why? Because, now unified they are twice as strong. One thing unification does is give a nation a better chance to compete with the rest of the world. Well, the same thing happened when England and Scotland got together.

Now, drop down a line in your notes. and let's narrow our scope to the parties within the Parliament: the Whigs and the Tories. Several things are working to the advantage of the Whigs at this time. First of all, they are able to take advantage of some serious blunders made by the Tories. Now, what mistakes could they possibly make?

The Treaty of Utrecht is one. Remember we talked about the War of the Spanish Succession? This was the treaty that ended that war, and it was written by the Tories. You wouldn't think that could hurt them, but it does. Let me tell you how:

The treaty gives England a lot of territory that belonged to the French and the Spanish: Hudson Bay, part of Canada,

Gibraltar (that rock that blocks entry and exit from the Mediterranean). The treaty also gives the English the Right of Asciento. That's a Spanish term and it means that England now has the right to trade with Spanish colonies. Foreign countries have never been legally allowed to do this before. The treaty says England can trade with them once a year, using one ship. Well, England breaks that agreement: she trades with the colonies once a year all right, but not with one ship—with one *fleet!* The goods they are trading are primarily slaves. England becomes the main provider of slaves for the Spanish colonies.

Now, how can this be a blunder for the Tories? you ask. It's a blunder, because the English people are not at all happy with the treaty. After such a long war, they felt that they should have received much more, and they are unhappy with the Tory party.

A second blunder committed by the Tory party is their opposition to the new German family that comes to the throne. Many Tories support a rebellion against George I in 1715. When the uprising is put down, George I no longer trusts the Tories.

O.K., drop down another line in your notes. I know, this is complicated, but your're doing just fine. While we're getting ready to shift gears, let's look more closely at the Hanovers, particularly George's personality and that of his son who eventually inherits the throne.

George I is a true-blue German. He won't learn English, and he hates England. In fact, he spends most of his time in Germany. He really doesn't like anything about England, including English women.

Student: If he didn't like England, why did he take the job?

Jim: Who saw the movie, *King Ralph?* Well, then you know that the opportunity to become the ruler of a rich country doesn't come along too often. Basically, George I wants the position so he can use the power to help his own German state.

When George I comes to the throne, he is married to an unusually intelligent and witty woman—sort of a modern liberated woman. She's the kind who likes to make smart remarks that George has to think about. Since George is not faithful to her, she decides she doesn't have to be faithful to him. That's right: they both mess around. The problem is the double standard at that time. It was O.K. for husbands to mess around, but not for wives.

So what does George do? He locks his wife up in a castle in Germany for thirty-two years and brings two mistresses to England with him. It's hard to understand his preference in women, because he brings two extremes: one who is very fat and one who is very skinny. In fact, the English call them "The Elephant" and "The Maypole."

George has another problem: he hates his son. There's an intense rivalry between them. Everyone in George's government wants to stay on his good side, but they also know that his son will eventually replace him and they don't want to get on the son's bad side. They don't know which George (I or II) to please.

But there is one man who has the skill to play both sides, father and son. His name is Robert Walpole, a special— some might say, untrustworthy—kind of politician. We're going to look at Robert Walpole tomorrow and see how he manages to manipulate both Georges.

When I completed my observations of Jim's classes, I knew I had seen only a small part of his practice. For example, I did not see him teach his AP students how to write essays; this occurred early in the fall semester. I also wished I knew more about the kinds of assignments he gives each class.

However, during my final hour of observation, as I looked around Jim's classroom at students who were clearly relaxed and at home, it suddenly occurred to me that perhaps the essence of Jim's practice was his efforts to meet his students' needs. He met their needs on several levels (physiological, psychological, and academic): that is, by allowing his students to bring food into his classroom, by transforming history into an entertaining serial, by providing the security of a solid knowledge base, by giving them clear expectations and paternal guidance, by helping them get good grades, and by providing parental affection. I wondered if he was aware of this theme.

What Jim's Students Told Me

Jim requested that I interview his students about his teaching, so a few days after my last observation, he left me alone with one of his regular American history classes. After introducing myself, I explained that I wanted to obtain the students' answers to two questions: What made Mr. Chesnut a good teacher? What kinds of teaching methods do you prefer? I drew a distinction between "traditional" ways of teaching, like lecturing, storytelling, and dictating notes; and "fun activities" like group discussions, role playing, and simulations. I set my audio cassette on "record," and prepared myself for a a heated debate.

Instead the students seemed to regard both questions as simple-minded and proceeded to put them to rest in less than ten minutes. The gist of their argument was summarized by one young lady when she said, "It's not the method that matters, it's the teacher." They frankly didn't care how a teacher presented academic material so long as it was clear. They prized teachers who demonstrated patience and concern that they were acquiring the knowledge needed to pass important tests, like the new state graduation exam.

Jim was a good teacher, because he cared about them and made every effort to help them succeed. His stories did, indeed, make history more interesting, but this was of minor importance; they didn't particularly want or expect to be entertained in class. Teachers who did not focus on material for which students would be held accountable (on state or national tests or later in college) were described as having an attitude of, "I've got mine (a paycheck)—who cares if you get yours."

My next task was to uncover some of the cognition and values beneath Jim's teaching. I gave him my description of his classes and the same list of questions I had given Laura.

Five days later Jim began to answer those questions during a ninety-minute interview which I audiotaped.

The Cognition Underlying Jim's Practice

On a sunny Monday morning in early March, Jim and I walked around the campus of Central High with a small audio cassette recorder. Eventually we settled on some bleachers overlooking the softball field, and I asked Jim how he arrived at his present teaching style; what had influenced it and how it had evolved. He was stumped for an answer:

"I've always envied colleagues who can think back to their childhoods and remember teachers who made real impressions on them. I've never been able to do that. I can recall a couple of teachers in junior or senior high whom I liked because they had personalities that came across well, but I can't recall their teaching styles. My memories of social studies classes consist mostly of working on assignments in the textbook or maybe reading aloud from the text. That particular style of teaching never appealed to me.

"I know I had good teachers, but I just can't recall them. You have to understand that when I was in high school I was very much like the students I have now. Social studies was just another required course, nothing I particularly liked. There were too many other school activities that took my attention. It really wasn't until I went to college and had to pick a career that I even thought about education."

In a way education was a natural career choice for Jim, because he had so many teachers in his family: a grandmother, mother, aunt, father, two sisters, and a brother-in-law. However, when he entered the University of Alabama, Jim had plans to become a career army officer. He gravitated to a major in education because of his contact with teachers, but he never planned to use it as a career.

To his surprise, he discovered that military service did not suit his temperament. After three and a half years, he left the army and sought an appointment teaching overseas through the Department of Defense. He did obtain an overseas assignment, but with an independent school system in Honduras, where he taught for two years and met his wife-to-be.

In 1976 he returned to Tuscaloosa, accepted a position in the city school system, and shortly thereafter began work on a master's in education. For the first four years, he taught American and European history to tenth and eleventh graders in a predominantly black high school. In 1980, when courts ordered integration abolished that school and established Central High, Jim moved to one of its campuses where he has been until today.

Jim's perceptions of the merits of a teaching career have matured since the years he served in the military. Instead of concerning himself with concrete benefits, he values teaching because of the intellectual and psychological gratification it provides through his association with young people:

"I like it so much and enjoy my association with kids so much that present teaching conditions would have to become extremely unattractive for me to ever give up this profession. Time, money, and workload are not issues for me. In fact, I probably work a lot harder as a teacher than I would in any other sector of civilian life."

When I asked Jim what particular aspects of his temperament made him suited for teaching, he was hard pressed for an answer and suggested that I ask his students:

"I guess mainly I try to keep my word and be as fair as possible with students. In fact, I'm more than fair: I provide numerous opportunities and options for improving their grades. Although this results in more work for me, it increases students' exposure to the subject matter. If a student fails to grasp the material on his first encounter with it, I try not to simply penalize him or her and move on to other material. Instead I give the student additional opportunities to master the material, even if this requires a second or third attempt and the doubling of work for me."

As Jim spoke, it became clear that being a military officer and being a classroom teacher were not unrelated vocations. Both required leadership, but Jim saw crucial differences in that leadership: "In the military, everything was right or wrong. If an individual made a mistake, I had to be uncompromising as his commanding officer and exact a penalty that might range from losing a monthly paycheck to serving time in jail. I had to do that, but I didn't enjoy it. I can be just as demanding in my own way with kids in high school, have just as many high expectations, but not have to create conflict or shatter egos. It involves the same degree of exactness and expectation, but I have more control over the options I can use."

One can see the theme of "military" discipline in Jim's style of teaching: his strong emphasis on order and organization. He could not recall how his style has evolved over the years, but knew he always tried to avoid presenting material as it appears in textbooks: cut-and-dried, a list of names and dates.

"I want students to know those basic facts," he said, "but I prefer to put them into a story format so there's some meaning and order to history. I tend to use the chronology of presidential elections as my anchor, my stepping-stones through American history. It allows me to digress, to spin off into side themes and return to the next election. I want to make the content accessible to students, yet put it on a level that is elevated enough to make them stretch. I want to see them grow as they acquire information, grow in writing and thinking skills."

Contrary to what I expected. Jim does not feel that high school students or schools have changed greatly over his eighteen-year career: "Maybe they have different problems and are not as able to organize their thoughts, but high school students seem about the same in terms of temperament and attitude." Similarly, Jim does not see any substantive changes in the quality of student teachers that the university sends to him. He has worked with at least sixteen over the past eight years.

As a teacher, Jim's primary goals have not changed either: "When they leave my class in May, I hope that my students realize that I genuinely liked and respected each of them. When I first meet my kids at the beginning of the school year,

I try to explain that we are involved in a cooperative program. What we are going to try to accomplish in my class will be the result of a fifty-fifty partnership. We each have our responsibilities.

"They want good grades, and I want to help them earn them, but good grades are not as important to me as knowing that I have exposed them to the historical knowledge our society expects them to have. I want to feel that I haven't shortchanged them.

"I give students the opportunity to acquire that knowledge, but what they choose to do with it is their business. It irritates me when university professors try to blame their freshman classes' lack of historical knowledge on high school social studies teachers. It's so easy to say we are not preparing students for college, but when students leave my class—or the classes of any of the other social studies teachers in my department—they have been exposed to the material they need. It's their job to learn it. There's a point at which students must be accountable for learning, not just teachers."

Jim appears to have no special biases or perspectives about history, but says he simply tries to present it evenly and fairly. That lead me to wonder why he chose history as his content field, and Jim explained that as a child he liked to read stories about heroes:

"It's not a great transition to go from mythical heroes and warriors to the heroes of history, such as Washington, Lincoln, or MacArthur. All you are doing is shifting to the realm of reality which makes the narratives even more interesting."

Clearly it is the notion of leadership that captured Jim's imagination at an early age: leadership as it affects history and, on a more personal level, being a commanding officer over enlisted men. One can see how this theme was simply modified for the classroom, as Jim now assumes the leadership of youngsters. Thus, it is no accident that Jim's definition of a good leader is also his definition of a good teacher: "An honest individual who deals fairly with others; who lives up to his word."

Jim's conception of teacher as leader has many implications. One is the belief that there is more to school than academic work. Jim spoke sadly of his own two children, an eleven-year-old son and a twelve-year-old daughter, who began to dislike school when they started junior high. Jim sees them being overwhelmed with academic work that saps their vitality and crowds out other important activities like athletics and clubs.

Unlike some educational reformers who would like to see the school year extended in hopes of making American society more competitive, Jim would like to see class periods shortened (regardless of the length of the school year) to make room for nonacademic electives that help students develop well-rounded personalities.

Teacher as leader also implies that one's primary commitment is not solely to one's content field but to the development of complete individuals: "Of course a teacher needs to know the subject he is responsible for, but a good teacher is someone whose real attachment is to the students. When students are respected and valued as members of a class, they respond in kind."

To Jim the heart of classroom teaching is the ability to interact with kids, something that his own preservice teacher education program did not address. Reflecting upon his undergraduate program, he recalls boring foundations courses, like the Philosophy of Education, and highly theoretical methods courses. The former he characterized as "rites of passage" that weeded out those who were not highly motivated to be teachers. The latter he described as useless in helping him learn how to teach.

He said he taught himself how to teach by trial and error and was fortunate that he began with kids who let him repair the mistakes he made. What he learned was "a commonsense approach to dealing with individuals. You have to realize that you teach young people, not a subject like history or English. If you come to the classroom thinking you're there to teach your content field, you'll have a lot of problems. That's where many student teachers run into difficulties, and I'm not sure there's anything the university can do about it, except give preservice candidates more time practicing in real classrooms."

Finally, I asked Jim how he would feel if one of his own children expressed the desire to become a teacher. "Very, very pleased," he responded with a smile:

"Sometimes former students return to tell me that they are majoring in education, and I like to think I had some influence on that career choice. For me teaching is an outstanding profession, although I realize I work under enviable conditions.

"I work in a school system that is positive and supportive of both teachers and students. My building administrators are professional and work hard to create an atmosphere that is so conducive to learning, it is impossible for any single unmotivated teacher to destroy it. They respect and cherish young people, regardless of race or socioeconomic background, and they believe that each child deserves a quality education.

"It's hard to explain exactly how I feel. I don't feel intrinsically superior to any of my students; some are probably smarter than me and as adults will earn more money than me. I have no desire to wield power or to make their lives difficult. I respect them and want to help them acquire the basic knowledge of American history that they are expected to have.

"But once I present that knowledge, it's their responsibility to retain and use it. If students want to throw it away, that's their choice. You know, we had a record number of students fail the math or language sections of the Alabama High School Graduation Exam this year. It's so easy to blame high school teachers for that, and it's easy for high school teachers, in turn, to blame elementary teachers.

"My wife is an elementary teacher, and I know how hard she works to motivate her students. If a child chooses to spend his or her time watching MTV instead of reading, as you and I did when we were kids, that's the child's choice. To a degree, I believe that it's the child's responsibility to learn."

By this Jim did not mean that teachers are not responsible for educating and motivating students, but that the problem and the solution must be viewed in a larger context:

"It's not just the teacher's job to motivate students; it's everyone's job: parents, religious leaders, civic leaders—

above all, students themselves. When the motivation and
the learning do not occur, society makes teachers the scape-
goats."

Although Jim did not use the word, he was also talking
about the need for children to grow up with a sense of self-
discipline. Once again I was reminded of an officer's role in
promoting character and discipline among those he would
lead.

Almost two hours had passed since we began talking, and
I thanked Jim for letting me take so much of his time. "I just
hope some of that made sense," he said as we began walking
back to the school. "It didn't come out exactly the way I
wanted it to."

"Don't worry," I assured him. "I'm going to transcribe this
tomorrow and give it back to you for editing by the end of
the week. I think you may be pleasantly surprised."

Jim laughed: "That's going to take a little bit of magic
on your part. In the meantime I think I'll check on Craig
[Jim's student teacher] and see how he's doing."

Jim headed for the entrance to the school, I for my car.
I was to interview Liza, the professor who teaches the social
studies methods course, in seven days, and I was trying to
imagine what she would say. A description of that interview
appears in the following chapter.

CHAPTER 6

LIZA'S COURSE ON METHODS OF TEACHING SECONDARY SOCIAL STUDIES

Cooperating teachers rarely forbid student teachers to try new things, but the student teachers get the message: traditional methods work better.

Liza joined the Department of Curriculum and Instruction at the University of Alabama in the fall of 1991, returning home to her family and the site of her own undergraduate education. She earned her doctorate in Louisiana where she taught social studies in grades 7–12 for three years and served as sponsor for many intramural activities. She taught a variety of subdisciplines (state and world history, geography, civics, etc.) to students ranging from the learning disabled to the gifted. At the end of her second year of teaching, she received the Teacher of the Year Award, based upon recommendations of students, parents, teachers, and administrators.

Her most recent experience in secondary classrooms was four years ago, when she decided to pursue a career in higher education, because she wanted to improve the quality of teaching she saw around her. This was her fourth year teaching secondary social studies methods. She was in the process of organizing a support group for pre- and in-service social studies teachers in Tuscaloosa: a forum for discussing problems and issues.

I interviewed Liza in her office at the university, which was sparsely furnished with a few photographs and a recently deceased plant. Somewhat diffident, Liza needed constant probing to elicit her pedagogical beliefs. I began by asking her whether secondary schools in Tuscaloosa had changed much since she was an undergraduate nine years ago.

"In some cases, very much so," she answered. "The climate of some schools has degenerated and students seem less respectful of teachers."

Liza's pedagogical beliefs were influenced early in her undergraduate program by two university professors who stressed the advantages of "living history" and experiential learning. Liza acquired the theoretical foundation for that approach during her doctoral study. During the interview she continuously stressed that she tries to mitigate theory with practical insights she gained as a secondary social studies teacher, making conscious efforts to embed her methods course in "the realities of classroom life." She said that she welcomes input from the experienced teachers who work with her methods students and student teachers.

Liza's methods course has not changed greatly over the past four years, but the longer she is away from the secondary classroom, the more compelled she feels to remind her students of certain realities: the heavy paperwork, the many time constraints, the need to prepare for several different teaching assignments, the special needs of students, and the need to build students' self-esteem. She said that she tries to convey "the heart of teaching" to her methods students. Her course is divided roughly into four components: the curriculum of social studies and its attendant theory; the subdisciplines and modes of presentation; instructional planning and class management; and a brief clinical experience.

Initially Liza asks her students to generate their own personal versions of ideal social studies curricula: what topics and skills do they think one ought to teach to secondary students in social studies classes? Liza follows this discussion with an examination of actual social studies curricula in Alabama and neighboring states. She also provides her students with examples of proposed curricular changes. At this point she introduces some of the theory underlying the study of social studies: for example, the need to teach content in ways that promote critical thinking and active citizenship.

After discussing the curriculum, Liza moves to the subdisciplines of social studies: history, geography, economics, sociology, and anthropology. Instructional objectives and methods of presentation are examined within each sub-discipline. Liza stresses active instructional formats, like cooperative learning and simulations, but is careful to embed these models in the content by giving her students sample lesson plans written by seasoned teachers and former methods students.

During the brief field experience, her students meet with experienced social studies teachers for three one-hour sessions, during which they discuss how teachers design instructional units and plan for daily instruction. Over the next two months, her students then complete three to five observations of the experienced teachers. Finally, in groups of five, they teach one-week units to a secondary class.

When observing experienced teachers, Liza's students are told to focus on specific aspects of instruction: the nature of pupil's prior knowledge and interests, the atmosphere of the class and the school, techniques the teacher uses to maintain class control and present material. Each of Liza's methods students is required to keep a written journal in which he or she evaluates and reflects upon these observations. Her students are also asked to evaluate each other's classroom teaching.

While her methods students are completing their clinical experiences, they continue to meet at the university to discuss and compare their observations. The purpose of these discussions is to examine different classroom environments, forms of class management, and ways of presenting material. Liza also uses the observations as a vehicle for teaching why two teachers can use the same instructional technique but achieve very different results.

Liza wants her students to become aware of some of the contextual factors that can affect the outcome of instruction, particularly the care a teacher has taken to prepare his or her students for a certain instructional format, like cooperative learning. After watching seasoned practitioners, Liza's students are asked to describe how they would handle the same material or situation.

Liza includes four major assignments in her course. Her students must write two units of instruction: one on any topic and for any grade they choose, the other for the week they actually teach a secondary class. Each student is also given a profile of a hypothetical secondary class, and the student must explain in writing how he or she would present a particular topic to that class. Finally, each student must maintain a reflective journal, to which Liza responds with marginal notations. In addition to these assignments, Liza gives two tests which usually consist of scenarios describing particular secondary classes. Students must explain in writing how they would present particular units of instruction to these classes, relating their choices to curriculum theory.

In the process of traversing these components of her course, Liza tries to impress her students with a few basic principles. One is Liza's belief that social studies teachers need to go beyond the basics to teach higher-order and critical thinking:

"The goals of most curriculum guides are very low, very basic. I try to stress the need to go beyond the facts—the names and dates of history—to get kids to synthesize, compare, and question." To Liza, this is the real goal of social studies, not rote recall of facts.

A second principle she stresses is that "social studies teachers need to make their students active participants in learning. Kids' favorite description of social studies is 'boring.'

They don't see the need to study this subject, so teachers must demonstrate why social studies is useful and important. How do historical events connect to today's world? This means that kids' motivation to learn must be more than doing well on tests. Two or three weeks after a test, kids have usually forgotten the information they studied. But if you show them how information relates to something in their own lives, they are likely to remember it."

In order to motivate students, Liza believes that teachers must use a variety of stimuli and instructional formats: "Routines may help manage a class, but they don't motivate kids to learn. A good teacher uses different devices, he or she surprises and motivates the kids to want to learn more. These don't have to be elaborate devices: sometimes a provocative question or an interesting photograph is enough to capture a child's imagination."

I asked Liza how she can tell good social studies teaching when she sees it:

"You can tell a teacher is good," she answered, "when kids are involved and excited about the material, when they're asking to know more. Where can they read more about the topic? Can they discuss it after class? Signs of poor teaching are students taking notes like robots, or maybe asleep with their heads on their desks; or classes motivated only by the threat of a test. Good social studies teaching is also using more than one mode of instruction. I know some social studies teachers who are gifted lecturers, but I think they need to use other modes as well in order to motivate kids."

One of Liza's favorite instructional methods is cooperative learning and group work: "I like cooperative learning, because kids learn social skills, they learn to be active participants, and they get to work on common goals with kids from different backgrounds. When students are given responsibility for their own learning, they usually become more involved in it."

Liza said that she realizes that learning these principles is different from understanding how to implement them in the classroom. Thus, she tries to help her methods students anticipate the planning involved in using these principles: the need to assemble materials, anticipate students' reactions, and work within severe time constraints.

Instead of using a textbook in her course, Liza has assembled a collection of articles, many of which were written by experienced social studies teachers who describe activities they have used. For example, in one article, a junior high school teacher explains how he taught geography:

Studies of oceans, lakes, and river systems can be taught
with the children approaching it as a vacation on the water,
as they pore over maps and charts to prepare their itinerary,
study about the places to visit, determine costs, and
examine what must be done to travel safely in this way.
Students not only learn about a place, but how to get there
and what to see and do. . . My pupils would study about an
area and plan an automobile trip through it, plot the route,
directions and distances to be traveled. time on the road,
and the amount and cost of gas. . .
(Kirman, 1988. p. 104)

Another way Liza tries to embed principles in practice
is by working through specific problems with her students:
"I ask them to think about how they would teach World War
II to secondary students. They begin by talking about the facts
they would teach—the names, events, and dates. Then I ask
them to consider how they could show pupils that the events
of the war shaped the world we live in today." Here Liza
suggests using oral histories, transcripts of interviews with
individuals who lived through the war. She also suggests
simulations: for example, having pupils enact the migration
of a Japanese-American family during the internment.

Liza explains to her methods students that the purpose
of such activities is to help pupils "live history," realize that
the people of the past had the same needs and emotions as
we do today. She points out that such activities can be used
with students of all academic abilities, not just the gifted.
To reinforce this point, she shows a video, *The Truth about
Teachers*, which showcases creative teachers in different
content fields and grade levels. The video (and Liza) stress
how these teachers are concerned about building their
students' self-esteem.

"The problem with ability grouping," Liza said, "is that
bright kids usually get to work on interesting activities, while
low-track kids get boring worksheets. If basic classes got to
do interesting things, they might learn more and enjoy
school." Liza also suggests to her students that some of these
activities can be used to assess student learning. Instead of
taking tests, pupils might write imaginary letters or journals

in which they describe historical events they have studied. To illustrate innovative assessment techniques, Liza has her methods students make maps out of salt and flour to demonstrate their knowledge of geography.

Liza's definition of a lesson plan used to be quite loose. but she now teaches the traditional format because students are expected to use it when they student teach (i.e., objectives, procedure, evaluation). She stresses the need to provide a motivating activity and some form of closure for each lesson.

Her definition of an instructional unit is broader: "I tell my students that there are many ways to create a unit: by using primary documents and no textbook; by enhancing a textbook chapter with outside resources and activities; and by staying completely with the text. I tell them that I don't endorse the latter option, but I am also honest about the time involved in preparing units for two or three teaching assignments. I see too many teachers constructing units around tests, making no attempt to connect the units. So I suggest ways that units can be connected with each other; then the curriculum makes sense."

Liza is also realistic about the utility of textbooks. She acknowledges their pervasive influence but retains a negative view of them: "They're dry, biased, and don't really go into topics in depth. They're getting better, but social studies teachers have to supplement them with other materials; it's up to a teacher to decide what parts are worthy of elaboration. That's just part of the decision making that goes into teaching. I know how overwhelming it is to have to prepare every day for two or three different teaching assignments, and I know how easy it is to fall back on a textbook with its end-of-the-chapter questions. But I try to get my methods students to remember the need to get kids involved; this is content that has no apparent value to them. Sticking to a textbook will not help involve them."

Liza often gets a chance to work with students after they have completed her methods course and begin student teaching. She said that they seem to remember what she has taught them, but that they do not always apply it in their classrooms. When they do, their attempts are sporadic. I asked her how she accounts for this:

"They're up against the routines that their cooperating teachers have established. Sometimes pupils don't want those routines interrupted, so they rebel against a student teacher who tries something new. In those cases I tell student teachers not to give up entirely; they shouldn't allow kids to dictate what they do. In other cases, I see student teachers modeling the techniques their cooperating teachers use. Cooperating teachers rarely forbid student teachers to try new things, but the student teachers get the message: traditional methods work better. Some student teachers try innovative activities, but if they don't work the first time, they're reluctant to try again. Instead they fall back on the standard routines already in place."

At the end of the interview, I asked Liza to evaluate the secondary social studies teachers she had seen in Tuscaloosa this year:

"They represent a wide range. There are some really great teachers using active strategies; then there are teachers who do the same things day after day but still manage to motivate kids. There are also some terrible teachers whose kids don't learn and don't behave; their classes are a waste of time for everyone."

I asked her what single piece of advice she would like to give to social studies teachers. and this is what she said:

"I would tell them not to let themselves be destroyed by the many negative variables associated with teaching: the lack of social respect, the heavy paperwork. I would remind them that they are important. I see too many teachers who are burnt out, waiting to retire because they have such a low sense of self-efficacy. Without support and resources, they feel they cannot really accomplish anything. That's why I always tell my methods students to try to create small support groups with other teachers. They must help each other remember that teachers really can accomplish important things."

At the conclusion of the interview, I gave Liza a copy of my narrative describing Jim's classroom practice (sans the cognition underlying it). A week later I was back in her office, this time interviewing her about the narrative.

Liza Evaluates My Description of Jim's Classroom Practice

Like Beth, Liza had made annotations in the margins, as she read the narrative. She began by reviewing these. Also like Beth, she tried to emphasize the positive things she saw in Jim's teaching, including: his attempts to create a special environment for students; his habit of reviewing the prior day's material before beginning the day's lesson; his many attempts to connect history to his own life experiences, those of his students, and current events. She also liked the way he adapted instruction for his regular (as opposed to AP) classes.

"His students obviously respect him," she said. "He makes them feel important and, in turn, they feel that the material he gives them is important."

It took many leading questions to get Liza to admit she had "some concerns." For example, she wondered about Jim providing the only interpretation of historical events:

"What if a student has a different perspective? Would he or she be judged incorrect? Do students have opportunities to disagree with Jim and give him feedback? I would like to see them express themselves more. I would also like to see students provided with a greater variety of stimuli and resources, like primary documents, photographs, videos, simulations—activities that involve kids.

"I also wonder about the difference between the tests Jim gives his AP versus regular classes. It seems that the more able students get interesting essays to write, while the basic students get only short-answer tests. This relates to what I said before, about how academic work for low-track students is usually much less interesting than the work assigned to more academically able students. I wonder whether the kids in the regular classes will retain the information they learn for short-answer tests. Writing essays requires students to synthesize information, and that tends to increase long-term memory."

More generally, Liza addressed Jim's tendency to motivate learning with tests and grades: "I want students to get good grades and do well on tests, she said, "but I also want them to take the knowledge with them, to be motivated to pursue and enrich it outside the classroom by reading, visiting museums, or visiting historical landmarks. I was looking for small-group activities that might motivate students to do those things."

At this point, I asked Liza to pretend I were one of her methods students. We have just spent four months learning why social studies should be active and participatory, and I have just observed Jim—an outstanding teacher who has won several awards. Could Liza explain why I didn't see him use any of the activities we learned about in her course?

Liza was clearly uncomfortable with that question and began by qualifying her answer: "I can't know Jim's motivation for not using certain techniques. I can only speak hypothetically about teachers, in general. Cooperative learning and other activities take a great deal of time to prepare. They also take a lot of time to execute. To some teachers it may seem a lot easier and faster just to give students the information; it's much harder to create situations where students discover it for themselves. Other teachers may be worried about the time involved and fear that they may not be able to cover as much content. Then there's the issue of discipline and class control. Switching to group work can cause problems.

"Any of these factors can put teachers off, but they're misapprehensions. In fact, you can use cooperative learning and other activities safely *and* cover content. I tell my methods students not to expect success the first time they use any technique. Kids are not used to it, and there may be some management problems at first; but that doesn't mean teachers' shouldn't try new methods."

"Are you saying that experienced teachers know about these alternative methods but that they have misconceptions that prevent them from using them?" I asked.

Liza thought a moment: "Yes, I think that if they had a chance to learn the truth about them, perhaps a chance to try them, they'd use them. I used them in my own secondary social studies classroom and found that they worked well and that my students performed as well as other classes on standardized tests. It didn't prevent them from acquiring factual material."

This led me to ask another question: "You say that getting students actively involved in class makes learning more fun and more effective. If that's true, then why do students like the way Jim teaches? And why do many other students seem to prefer the traditional, information-giving style of teaching?"

"First of all," Liza responded, "Jim doesn't lecture. He has a real gift. He makes history alive and relevant, but few teachers can do that. Most teachers who assume the role of information giver just slap transparencies overhead and tell their students to copy information into their notes. They don't bother to elaborate or connect history to the students' own lives."

"Then why don't you teach your methods students about storytelling history?" I asked.

"But I do. We talk about four ways to teach history: the Storyteller; the Eclectic, who uses different methods; the Cosmic Philosopher, who emphasizes how history affects everyone; and the Relativist Reformer, who looks at events critically, analyzing how they have changed our lives. I'm not against any one method of teaching social studies; I just tell my students to vary their methods."

I tried another approach: "Which way do you think high school students prefer to be taught social studies? Given two equally talented teachers, would most students prefer a lecture/storytelling style or group activities?"

"It depends on the students," Liza answered. "If they have never been exposed to group activities, they may fear that they will not get the information they need to do well on state or national exams. Like teachers, students may have misconceptions about those methods."

"Are you saying that if students really understood those methods, they would prefer them to the traditional information-giving style of teaching?"

Liza remained silent for a moment, reluctant to commit to an answer, so I pressed on: "What would you say to Jim if he claimed that your alternative, active methods would prevent him from covering the required curriculum?"

That apparently struck a chord: "I don't accept that," Liza said. "You can cover just as much material with group activities as you can by giving information. A teacher must decide initially which parts of the curriculum he or she wants to emphasize. That is, you have to decide what you think is most important for the kids to know. If anything, most social studies teachers probably try to cover too much material in great detail. That's why students usually reach the university never having covered contemporary history in any of their high school classes. One solution to this would be to teach history in reverse chronology."

I pressed Liza again: "Won't students be penalized if a teacher doesn't teach to the required curriculum? They're the ones who must do well on entrance exams."

"Well, I would suggest that teachers need to become more involved in writing the curriculum they are forced to teach. I tell that to my methods students all the time. Until and unless teachers become active in the process, they'll always be forced to adhere to someone else's idea of the curriculum. At some point teachers need to say, 'It's not just the quantity of knowledge that matters, it's also the quality—how that knowledge is taught: depth versus breadth.'"

I asked Liza whether her methods students ever asked her to account for the inconsistencies between her course and the teaching they observed in secondary classrooms: "Not really," she said. "We discuss what they see, but I can't recall students ever asking me to explain inconsistencies. I try to help them understand the pressures that often constrain teachers and how that may account for what they observe in schools."

"Are you implying that, if one could remove those constraints, experienced teachers would rush to use the activities you advocate?" I asked.

Liza thought a minute before answering: "I think so, providing those teachers believed that their students would be responsive and that they (the teachers) would enjoy the activities. Yes, if teachers had the time and resources needed, and if they felt their students would respond positively, I think that they would use activities and small groups. It would make their job easier, because those techniques give kids opportunities to learn as well as have fun."

Liza ended the interview with a final concern: "I worry about the student teachers who are placed with Jim. What if they try to transfer his storytelling method into their own classes but don't have his talent. There's a very real possibility that they would turn his style into dull lecture. Student teachers may not have the talent to use his style or they may not see the differences between storytelling and lecturing.

"Also, do his student teachers know where he gets his synthesis of history? Does he tell them what resources he consults and how he arrives at a 'story'? He obviously uses more than their textbook. Every student teacher needs to find a method that fits his or her personality; that means they need a chance to try many different methods in class."

I asked Liza what she did in her methods course to help novices get in touch with their own classroom personalities. She mentioned the reflective journals her students must keep, noting feelings and reactions to concepts they learn and behaviors they observe in classrooms. Liza responds to them in the margins.

It was obviously difficult for Liza to be critical of Jim, whom she admired, and she was relieved when the interview ended. Despite my many hours conversing with Jim, I couldn't guess how he might respond to her comments. A week later, after Jim had a chance to read and digest this chapter, I found out.

CHAPTER 7

JIM'S RESPONSE TO LIZA

There's very little practical application for much of what is taught at the university."

At first Jim had great difficulty responding to Liza's chapter. Part of the reason for this was his obvious desire not to criticize Liza on a personal level. However, as our discussion turned to the nature of "good teaching," how one learns to teach, and the most appropriate role a university might play in that process, it became clear that Jim had great difficulty finding the words he needed to express his most deeply felt beliefs.

Back at our spot on the bleachers late on a Friday afternoon, Jim began by making some very general observations about university course work:

"There's very little practical application for much of what is taught at the university. Instead of all that theory, I wish they would provide students with more practical applications: teach them about the legal rights and responsibilities of teachers according to state and district guidelines; teach them how to keep an accurate register. These are relatively simple skills, but they're crucial and—like many other practical aspects of teaching—they're ignored by the university. Novices also need to be familiar with curriculum guides for various states and school districts. Of course, I realize that if these suggestions were followed, you'd have to reduce the number of theory courses by half."

While Jim commended Liza for attempts to give her students concrete examples of inductive methods, Jim noted the inconsistency between what education professors preach and what they usually practice; namely, they endorse inductive teaching methods but rarely use them in their own classes.

Jim added: "A large problem is that university professors expect preservice candidates to transplant methods derived from research directly into secondary classrooms. When they try to do that, the methods often fall apart. This is an unforgiving environment," Jim added, gesturing toward the school.

"Not that a teacher is threatened in the halls or in his classroom, but it's easy for a novice teacher to fall victim to what I call the 'Guppy Syndrome.' That's the tendency of students to 'consume' teachers and students they perceive as weak. When student teachers try different methods, often failing, they can appear weak and tentative. Their behavior lacks consistency, routines (a word I shudder to use, because professors regard routines with such contempt).

"But students look for routines; without them, they feel no anchor, no guiding structure."

I found that observation fascinating, I told Jim, because— according to the university perspective—one of the best things a teacher can do is *avoid* consistency and routines.

Jim smiled at this: "But school life revolves around standard routines: routines administrators expect of teachers and routines that students expect of teachers. When the bell rings, students *want* a teacher who says, 'Let's get down to work now. Take out your notebooks and let's review what we discussed yesterday.' Routines give students security and direction. I'm sorry, but I think students are generally not comfortable with unstructured, nondirect teaching."

Here Jim described a special American Studies program at Central High which is designed to meet the needs of the minority of students who tolerate and succeed in an unstructured academic environment. It's a very creative program in which students are largely self-directed in their learning.

Jim pointed out that the students who elect American Studies in the eleventh grade are not necessarily brighter than others, just temperamentally suited to this alternative form of learning. "What I find interesting," Jim said, "is that about half of the kids who elect American Studies in the eleventh grade choose to return to structured classes in the twelfth grade."

Again I couldn't help interrupting Jim: "This is fascinating, because the methods most highly regarded by methods professors, like Beth and Liza, are those that are inductive and relatively unstructured: 'discovery teaching' in which information is not given by the teacher but elicited from the students. According to Liza, if students and teachers truly understood those inductive methods, they would be used more widely in secondary classrooms. I gather you don't agree with that."

"No," Jim responded. "In my social studies department I think that teachers have an adequate understanding of discovery learning, cooperative learning, and the other methods Liza teaches; but they choose not to use them because their students would not tolerate that style of instruction. You know, it's curious, but even university students dislike inductive and indirect styles of teaching. Taking an unstructured course is like wandering out into an open field and not knowing in which direction to go. The teachers I regarded as best in my high school and college careers organized content efficiently and presented it as directly as possible."

Was Jim suggesting that the presentation of academic content was an issue much simpler than distinctions among pedagogical methods: that is, that it was simply a matter of organizing information logically and directly? "Jim, are you saying that pedagogical method really doesn't matter?"

Jim had a hard time responding to that. He thought for several minutes: "It matters to some degree, but teaching method is not as simple as most methods professors think it is. It depends a great deal on how successfully a teacher can use a particular method. Take Craig [Jim's student teacher], for example. He's tried to use my storytelling technique, but it doesn't quite work for him; it lacks vitality and spark. That's because it is not his own style; that will emerge naturally in its own time.

"Methods professors like Liza plant seeds: some are sterile and never bloom. But some are taken up by student teachers and planted in secondary classrooms, where they experiment with them. This is not a neat or direct transplantation, and professors need to realize that. Some of the methods they teach will not necessarily work in secondary classrooms.

"Each method must be adapted for the particular teacher and the individual classroom context. Instead of acknowledging that, university professors seem to be preoccupied with labeling some pedagogical methods as 'good' and others as 'less good.'"

"At last," I gloated. "Now I get to ask the question I've been dying to ask: what do you think is the best method for teaching social studies?"

"What do you mean by, 'best method'?" Jim shook his head and spluttered for a few minutes. "I suppose any method that allows a teacher to present information to students in a way they can understand. How can there be better or worse methods, when it depends upon a particular teacher's success in using them? Storytelling history is best for me, but it may not be best for Craig because of his unique temperament, personality, or tone of voice. I expect that when he gets his own classes, he will reject, modify, or supplement the methods he saw me model."

Jim shook his head again. "No methods are inherently better or worse than others. University professors tell us in no uncertain terms that lecture is inherently worse, and they don't want to see student teachers using it. If lecture is so bad, why do so many excellent teachers use it? I've had teachers who used direct methods and those who used indirect ones, and that's not what made them good or bad teachers. Method is overshadowed by personality and rapport."

Was Jim suggesting that, at any level of education, what students get out of a course has less to do with pedagogical technique than it does with the teacher's personality, values, and sense of commitment?

"You bet," he said. "Above all, it has to do with the sense that the teacher is there for the students. We've talked about this before, Dona: the rapport between a teacher and his or her students. It's an aspect of teaching virtually ignored by university course work. The university never teaches candidates about being sensitive and relating to pupils; I can tell, because that's where student teachers usually experience the biggest problems. I've observed a number of student teachers who got excellent grades in courses, mastered content knowledge, but had no idea of how to relate to kids. And that's something that kids sense immediately. It's also something I can sense immediately about student teachers."

Here I invited Jim to describe the best ways a university might help novices learn to "read" and respond to pupils.

"The best thing a university could do is expose them to secondary classrooms, not just as observers but as performers; and require proportionately less time in university courses. I'll be perfectly honest with you: when the university sends preservice candidates to my classroom as part of some clinical experience [other than student teaching], I and many other teachers tend to use them to do xeroxing and grading. I give them very little opportunity to perform as teachers. I would like to see a laboratory school specifically designed to give novice teachers opportunities to teach to real secondary students in genuine classroom environments."

Jim was also honest in admitting that he would not volunteer to work in such a laboratory school, because he hates to relinquish his classes to teachers-in-training. As we spoke, Jim was coming to the end of a two-week period in which his student teacher had assumed teaching duties for all his classes. This is a state requirement in Alabama, and Jim was "desperate" to get his classes back:

"It's not that Craig hasn't been doing a fine job. It's just that I'm miserable when I'm not teaching. I need the nourishment I get by associating with kids. I think I'd die without my classes. I work with the university's teacher education program, because I feel obligated to do so. If seasoned teachers hadn't allowed me to practice in their classrooms when I was learning, I would have been lost. So now I feel that I owe the same thing to a new generation of teachers. But I hate giving up my classes, and I hate to see my kids subjected to a lot of experimentation. At the same time, I realize it is important for novices like Craig to be able to experiment. and I try to encourage him to do so."

Jim had now touched on another issue I was particularly interested in exploring: what sorts of advice or information did he give to his student teachers?

Very little, as it turned out. Because he is so sensitive to the need to individualize teaching style, Jim is reluctant to give specific advice. Instead, he said that he tries to alleviate the fears and misconceptions student teachers often harbor and tells them to expect that some of their experimentation will fail. Some of the methods taught by professors will not work. Student teachers must recognize when they are not working and move on to something else: "Don't stay with a sinking ship."

Inevitably Jim sees student teachers gravitate to a lecture style because of the pressure to cover a certain amount of material. Contrary to Liza's contention that a teacher can cover as much ground with inductive methods as he or she can with direct methods, Jim has seen the slow pace of discovery learning conflict with the need to stick to an efficient schedule:

"It's just the reality of schools: it is of paramount importance to provide students with the information and skills they need in a timely and efficient manner. The state and the district expect it; parents expect it; students expect it. Even the university expects it! Student teachers can experiment with whatever methods they like, as long as students receive and understand the information they need."

Again I probed: "Are you saying that method is not important?"

Jim sighed, "I guess I'm not making myself very clear. Look, what I'm saying is that no student teacher adopts the methods taught at the university or the methods modeled by a cooperating teacher." At this point Jim had to resort to figurative language:

"The university provides novices with theories about how to build a house. When student teachers come out here to secondary classrooms, they take those theories and begin to construct models of a house. Some of the models don't work; they collapse. But some do work, and those are the models that student teachers take into their first year of real teaching. There they try to build a real house. When they start to build, they find that they have to make adjustments and correct flaws overlooked in the model stage. As they make adaptations, new flaws appear and must be corrected. In the end, a novice teacher may combine two or three models into a special, one-of-a-kind house. It's a house that will work for only one person; only one person can live in it."

I asked Jim what he looks for in student teachers as they experiment with models, and again he spoke about rapport with pupils: "I look at their relationships with the kids; I look at their verbal and nonverbal language for evidence that they have established a rapport. I also look to see if content is clearly and efficiently organized. Most student teachers initially have trouble relating to kids, but I can sense if a novice has a true affection for kids and for this profession."

I was curious as to whether Jim had ever met a student teacher who he felt did not have the potential for establishing a rapport with kids, and his response took me by surprise:

"Given sufficient time and exposure to kids, anyone with a mastery of content can learn to be a competent teacher. Some take longer to acquire the skills and may never reach a level of expertise. I can't tell Craig or any other student teacher how to develop the skills. It will come naturally in its own time, as Craig experiments with his own students. He's got to build his own house with his own blueprints."

I was stunned at the implication: did Jim believe that *anyone* could learn to teach? Apparently, yes. In fact, he added: "If properly motivated and given enough time, I think anyone can master the skills needed to perform any profession."

However, Jim also draws a clear distinction between "standard" and "great" teachers:

"For standard teachers, teaching remains an 8:00 A.M.–3:00 P.M. job. They have no desire to participate in extracurricular activities or to associate with kids outside of school. They do what is required, and they get the job done, but they are not the great teachers who are remembered by students ten or fifteen years down the line: the teachers who change kids forever.

"Great teachers are great not just for what they do in the classroom, but for what they do outside of school. That might include taking kids camping or skiing over weekends or during the summer; working on the prom or Homecoming; coaching Scholar Bowl. Great teaching is a function of commitment and temperament: a genuine affection for kids and a commitment to making them well-rounded, healthy members of society.

"That's something that goes beyond academic achievement and the walls of a school; it cannot be contained between the hours of 8:00 A.M. and 3:00 P.M. I'm not sure it is something that can be taught. I think maybe the capacity to be a great teacher is a gift."

I asked Jim if he thought Craig had the capacity. "I don't know. He's a lot like me when I was that age: quiet, shy, uncomfortable around kids. It's funny, but now I've actually reached a point where I'm more comfortable around kids than adults (to tell you the truth, Dona, I'm just getting comfortable with you!). In a room full of adults, I want to sit in the back and disappear from sight. But I can't get enough of being around kids. In fact, my wife is starting to get very frustrated with me about that.

"I don't know how good a teacher I am. I probably don't follow the 'rules' about how teachers should relate to students. I kid too much with them. There's an equality in our relationship, yet they know I'm in control. My classes may be teacher-oriented, but the teacher is student-oriented. That's because I know that good teaching is in the eyes of the students."

Two hours had passed since the interview began. The sun was setting, and Jim suddenly realized he was late picking up his mother-in-law at the Birmingham Airport. As I packed up my cassette recorder, I suddenly remembered that Laura's husband liked to tease her with the observation that part of her had never grown up. I realized that this was undoubtedly true of Jim, as well, and explained why he found his interaction with students "nourishing." Teaching not only suited his personality and allowed him to provide a gentle form of leadership: it was the special, one-of-a-kind house he had built for the child in him who had never grown up.

CHAPTER 8

WHERE AND WHY
THE PROFESSORS AND
THE TEACHERS DISAGREED

---

*Dismissing the distinction between the two perspectives as
the result of socialization merely begs the issue. Cultures are
not constructed arbitrarily; in order to truly understand a
culture, one must probe the functional values of the beliefs
and behaviors associated with it.*

In writing this final chapter my objectives were to describe
fundamental differences between the perspectives of the
teachers and those of the professors, to speculate about the
functional values of those and to draw inferences about their
implications for preservice teacher education. It is important
to note that the conclusions presented in this chapter are
mine alone and that they represent *my interpretations* of the
observational and interview data included in prior chapters.
In some instances, Beth or Liza disagrees with my conclusions.

I began by identifying qualities common to and characteristic of the teachers' and the professors' discourse. I looked
for opinions and values that appeared consistently among the
teachers, among the professors, and between the teachers and
professors. I discovered that the data could be described in
terms of four general themes. These are detailed in the first
section of this chapter.

I then examined the content of the interviews that
I conducted with the two student teachers, looking for

.roborating evidence that the themes existed beyond my own perception. Although the student teachers did not describe differences between the university and school views in the same terms I used, they perceived many of the same discrepancies. These interviews are described in the second section of this chapter.

Although this is a small, interpretive study of four individuals, I was curious about the external validity of the themes I extracted. By this I mean the degree to which my conclusions and inferences might be generalized to other teachers (elementary as well as secondary), other professors, and the institutions they represent.

For evidence of external validity I turned to recent empirical and theoretical literature on teaching and teacher education. If one could find echoes of similar themes in this literature, one might reasonably assume that the themes were viable beyond the boundaries of this project. Thus the third section of this chapter, where findings are related to existing literature on teaching, is more than perfunctory conformity to the format of scholarship: it testifies to the generalizability of my conclusions.

I began this inquiry with a question: how could Laura and Jim be outstanding teachers and yet adhere to practices that are anathema to university methods professors? The data I collected suggest that the answer is profoundly simple: Laura's and Jim's definition of classroom teaching bears little resemblance to that of Beth and Liza. Although the teachers and the professors often used the same terminology to discuss classroom teaching and learning, to a large degree they seemed to be describing different phenomena. Indeed, comparing the two perspectives was like looking at maps of entirely different domains. In the final section of this chapter I discuss some of the implications of those discrepant maps.

Points of Difference: Comparing the Two Perspectives

Fundamental differences between the teachers' and the professors' views of classroom teaching and learning can be described in terms of four themes: teaching as a science versus a form of self-expression; the mechanism that accounts for student learning; the objectives of instruction; and an insider versus outsider view of schools.

Teaching as a Science Versus a Form of Self-expression

In reading Beth's and Liza's descriptions of their methods courses and their critiques of the teachers' practices, it became clear that both professors have stepped back from the experience of the classroom. As a result they now see classroom teaching in more abstract, objective, and scientific terms.

Each professor describes classroom learning in terms of a rational, linear process that is best explained by cognitive theories. Beth and Liza both appear to endorse a philosophy called "constructivism":

> Cognitive scientists today share with Piagetians a constructivist view of learning, asserting that people are not recorders of information but builders of knowledge structures. To know something is not just to have received information but also to have interpreted it and related it to other knowledge...[constructivism assumes] that the goal of all...instructional activities is to stimulate and nourish students' own mental elaborations of knowledge and to help them grow in their capacity to monitor and guide their own learning and thinking. (Resnick and Klopfer, 1989, pp. 3–4)

Inductive and discovery teaching techniques can be used to help pupils develop problem-solving skills and to integrate new information into their preexisting knowledge structures. Instead of dispensing information, a classroom teacher presents carefully designed problems and helps pupils find logical (not necessarily "correct") solutions. The motivation to learn becomes the fun of discovering solutions rather than preparing for a test.

Acquiring problem-solving skills takes precedence over covering the curriculum, and the social interaction inherent in group problem-solving reinforces learning. Much of the rationale (or "science") underlying constructivism is derived from cognitive studies of expert performance: that is, close comparisons of the thinking demonstrated by novice and expert practitioners in a variety of knowledge domains (Bransford and Vye, 1989).

For Liza, constructivism takes the form of simulations, role playing, and cooperative learning, activities that are supposed to promote critical thinking and learning outside as well as inside the classroom. For Beth, constructivism takes the form of a flexible and somewhat iconoclastic view of language that stresses utility and creativity rather than correctness. Beth refers explicitly to cognitive studies of how skilled authors compose, as means of justifying her pedagogical philosophy.

When asked why more teachers do not use such techniques, both professors cited constraints: the need to conform to curriculum guides, fear of having a noisy classroom, etc. If teachers truly understood methods consistent with constructivism, they would adopt them; and students would prefer them to the more traditional information-giving format. Students would learn more effectively and would be motivated to continue their learning outside the classroom.

Although Beth and Liza conceded that a teacher can override the shortcomings of pedagogical method by force of personality, this is clearly the exception (in their minds) rather than the rule. Each professor acknowledged the need for teachers to find methods that suit their personalities, but they also indicated that some methods are inherently superior to others. As Jim put it: lecturing is bad; inductive questioning is good.

The teachers' views stand in sharp contrast to this objective, scientific definition of teaching. Each teacher's practice is driven by affective, highly personal considerations; each has evolved an instructional style that is inextricably connected with his or her personality and life experiences. To Jim, teaching is a form of leadership particularly suited to his sensitivities. In the regimentation and order of his classroom, one can see lingering traces of his military aspirations: an emphasis on self-discipline, obedience, and building character. One can see this theme, too, in his tendency to interpret history as the result of decisions made by political and military leaders.

Laura's beliefs and practices emphasize the social correctness of language. To her, achieving according to the established rules of society is crucial; for being correct, achieving academically, is a tool of upward mobility—the power to attain financial and personal rewards. This is a lesson she learned early in life and which she now conveys to her students.

She sees her job as a teacher as that of helping her students compete; one does not find any of Beth's iconoclastic qualifications about correct language in Laura's discourse. Laura is not teaching her students to rebel or redefine standards; she is an academic coach committed to helping students succeed in life.

In Laura's classroom practice one can also see influences of some of her own teachers: the grammarian who drilled students and exacted perfect performances the teacher who outlined everything on the blackboard; the science teacher who illustrated how small concepts evolved into progressively larger ones. Laura eventually modified this template, just as she learned the benefits of being adaptable in life.

Laura and Jim entered teaching for very different reasons, and the paths that lead them to Central High are configured differently. However, they have something in common: each adapted a pedagogical model to suit his or her personality and values. In addition, both define the objectives of classroom instruction as extending beyond the purely cognitive.

Beth and Liza have not only objectified the task of classroom teaching, they have also narrowed its function to that of cognition: to help students acquire knowledge and problem-solving skills. To Laura and Jim, a teacher's job goes far beyond helping children achieve academically: it includes building children's self-esteem and self-discipline; teaching them to distinguish fact from opinion, to question their own values, and to interact effectively with individuals from different backgrounds. Promoting cognition and the acquisition of content knowledge represents a small part of what they want to accomplish with their students.

The Mechanism That Accounts for Learning in Classrooms

The most important aspect of classroom teaching, according to Beth and Liza, is the way in which academic material is presented: what is generally referred to as the *method* of teaching. Both professors made a clear distinction between teachers giving information to students or eliciting it from them via inductive techniques. Both professors believe that the former generally does not promote critical thinking, while the latter does.

To a degree, the professors also believe that teachers must entertain and motivate students, although I am sure they would prefer to express this belief in terms of making learning "intrinsically enjoyable." One of the best ways teachers can accomplish this is by avoiding consistency and routines and by varying pedagogical method.

Jim and Laura have a very different view of how learning occurs in classrooms. They see the presentation of academic material as a mere organizational task. As Laura put it: a teacher has a great amount of material that she must wade through, organize, and communicate efficiently. Thus, instead of "method," Laura and Jim speak of the "organization" of material, emphasizing only that it be logical and clear.

One can see this in Laura's practices of outlining information (on the blackboard or on transparencies) and dictating class notes. One can also see it in the careful structure Jim imposes upon his students' class notes. In organizing content, these teachers are not about to let their students make key decisions: that is, they do not adhere to the constructivist belief that students should arrive at their own, idiosyncratic organizations of new information. Laura and Jim also see consistent routines as essential to student learning: anchors that provide security and direction.

Instead of citing pedagogical method as the critical element of classroom learning, Laura and Jim talk about the texture of their interactions with students, collectively and individually. They see classroom learning as the result of countless student-teacher interactions that surround careful demonstrations and explanations. The importance of demonstration (modeling) can be seen in Jim's explanation of the process involved in answering document-based questions on the advanced placement history exam and in Laura's directions for creating sentences with particular grammatical structures. However, it is not just the demonstration that accounts for student learning, but how that demonstration is mitigated by a teacher's personality and interaction with students.

I do not mean to imply here that Beth or Liza ignore the importance of personality and rapport, or that Laura and Jim disregard the format of instruction. However, the professors clearly see pedagogical method as the *primary* variable, personality and the dynamics of personal interaction as secondary mitigating factors. The teachers believe the converse.

In this sense Beth and Liza focus on the form, or surface features of instructional presentation, while Laura and Jim emphasize the personal interdynamics underlying student-teacher interaction. It is interesting to note here that when Beth or Liza acknowledge the influence of the teacher's personality and rapport with students, it is expressed it terms of motivating students as opposed to helping them master content.

The Objectives of Classroom Instruction

On the whole, the professors are much more idealistic about the objectives of classroom instruction. Teachers are supposed to design lessons that make learning enjoyable rather than a chore; one does not teach to a test; one does not motivate with the threat of tests. Moreover, a teacher should adapt the required curriculum to the students' needs.

This stands in sharp contrast to Laura's and Jim's view of learning as the job of students. That is, they see students as having jobs that they must complete in order to succeed in life: namely, acquiring certain skills and information, getting good grades, passing state graduation exams or advanced placement tests, going on to compete in college.

Accomplishing these tasks allows students to succeed financially, socially, and psychologically. Laura and Jim are advocates and coaches, not entertainers or motivators. They expect much of the motivation to come from the students themselves.

The teachers are also quicker to cite social factors that affect their ability to teach students: the pervasive influence of television, familial pressures, etc. Jim made it especially clear that a teacher ought not to be expected to counteract such social factors; at some point a teacher's responsibility for students' learning stops and others (parents, students themselves, etc.) must be held accountable.

Moreover, Laura and Jim teach to the test, cover the curriculum, and apologize for neither. Indeed, they perceive these to be two of their primary tasks: to help students compete now and in the future. Neither teacher questions, subverts, or rebels against the system; instead they try to help students succeed within it. Interestingly, my discussion with one of Jim's classes and Laura's survey of her classes suggest that students' beliefs about the objectives of classroom instruction are consistent with those of the teachers rather than the professors.

The students appear to see classroom learning as an economic necessity, to see grades and tests as serious "business." Teachers who don't care, they told me, have an attitude of "I got mine—who cares if you get yours." Their belief seems more than mere socialization; these students are aware of the hard realities of life: the need to acquire high school diplomas and college degrees, the price one pays for a piece of the middle class. One detects no idealism in their perception of classroom learning. Perhaps this is part of what Laura sees as their "loss of innocence." Perhaps one would find different values among students from more affluent families.

An Insider Versus Outsider View of Schools

Laura and Jim fell into teaching accidentally or for extrinsic reasons. However, both stayed in the classroom, because teaching fit their respective personalities and values.

They are happy going to work each day; they like kids, classrooms, and schools; perhaps in part, because within each teacher there is a child who never grew up. Although there are probably aspects of schools they would like to see altered, one does not find dissatisfaction with the status quo in their discourse.

In contrast, both professors chose to leave the classroom: Beth, because she needed another kind of intellectual challenge: Liza, because she did not like much of the teaching she saw around her and wanted to be in a position to change it. In short, Beth and Liza did not fit, intellectually or politically. Like most of the education professors I have known, they are iconoclasts, outsiders who seek to change the nature of classroom instruction and schools.

This incendiary attitude permeates their rhetoric. One can see it in Beth's rejection of the purist view of language and in her advice to methods students about subtle ways of subverting the curriculum. One can see it in Liza's assertion that teachers should play a larger role in designing required curricula and the tests used to evaluate student learning. Both professors see much of the traditional structure of schools in terms of "constraints" that hamper teachers. Finally, both express cavalier attitudes about "teaching to the test" and "covering the curriculum." In this, they are not merely outsiders, but provocateurs.

Summary. The themes described above are summarized in Table 8.1. In the remaining sections of this chapter, I use the terms "professors'/university view" and "teachers' view" to refer to the opposing sets of tenets displayed in Table 3.

Interviews with the Student Teachers

To what degree were these two perspectives evident to student teachers who came through the secondary program at the University of Alabama? To answer that question, I interviewed two student teachers: Craig, Jim's current student teacher, and Betty, who was working with Laura (these are

Table 8.1
The Two Views of Classroom Teaching

Issue	The professors'/university view	The teacher's's view
Teaching as a profession	Teaching is a science based on cognitive/psychological theory and research.	Teaching is a form of self-expression that is highly personalized and subjective.
	It can be learned almost exclusively from university course work.	It cannot be taught directly. One learns to teach through trial and error during many hours of interaction with students in classrooms.
The objectives of a teacher	The emphasis is on cognition and the acquisition of academic skills.	The objectives are broader and include helping students develop self-esteem, social skills, and a healthy personality.
	Classroom instruction should be intrinsically enjoyable so as to motivate learning outside school.	Instruction should prepare students for tests, graduation exams, and college entrance exams. Teachers are not responsible for what students choose to do (or not do) with the skills they acquire in school; the students, their parents, and other members of society must share this responsibility.
	A primary objective of instruction is the development of critical thinking and a sense of ownership (of academic material) on the part of students.	Teachers are like coaches: their job is to help students compete for financial, social, and psychological success according to society's rules
		Much of what an effective teacher accomplishes with students occurs outside the classroom in the context of intra- and extramural activities.

Table 8.1 (cont.)
The Two Views of Classroom Teaching

Issue	The professors'/university view	The teachers's view
What accounts for student learning in the classroom	Pedagogical method: how academic material is organized and presented. A teacher's personality and rapport with students is a secondary, potentially mitigating factor.	The many small interactions that occur between a teacher and students (individually and collectively).
	It makes a crucial difference whether a teacher gives information or elicits it inductively; there are "better" and "worse" methods of presenting material.	The heart of teaching and learning lies in the teacher's rapport with students; this supercedes the influence of pedagogical method. How academic material is presented is a relatively commonsense task: it is important only that it be organized logically and clearly.
	An effective teacher uses a variety of pedagogical methods and does not adhere to consistent routines.	An effective teacher adheres to a set of instructional routines on which students can depend; routines facilitate learning.
	Student learning is the result of a logical, scientific instructional plan; in general, the success of a lesson can be predicted on the basis of the pedagogical method(s) employed by the teacher.	Student learning is inextricably connected with affect. It depends upon a teacher's success in communicating his or her affection, respect for, and commitment to students. It is idiosyncratic and generally not predictable. The path to student learning may be very different for individual students in the same class (due to personalities, family influences, etc.).

Table 8.1 (cont.)
The Two Views of Classroom Teaching

Issue	The professors'/university view	The teachers's view
Political advocacy	An attitude that often advocates radical changes in schools, curricula, and testing.	Generally endorses the status quo; if change is desired, it should be pursued through formal channels.
	Advises pre- and in-service teachers to take more control: for example, through quiet subversion or overt rebellion.	Accepts the rules and systems as they exist; the objective is not to change the system but to help students compete within it.

both pseudonyms). I asked each novice the following questions during a private interview:

1. What inconsistencies, if any, did you notice between what you were told during your methods course and what you found was practiced in secondary classrooms?

2. Which university courses, if any, provided you with useful information about teaching secondary students?

3. When you get your own classes in the fall, what pedagogical methods do you plan to use?

Jim's student teacher was relatively positive about his university course work which he described as "generally helpful." However, as soon as he began student teaching, he realized that few practicing teachers used inductive or discovery teaching methods that Liza introduced to him.

I asked Craig why he thought this was so, and he suggested two reasons: the amount of time required to prepare for those formats is prohibitive when one must prepare for more than one class assignment; those methods are inappropriate for some classes and some students. He felt that inductive methods would not be effective with classes that were difficult to control or with low-ability students.

Craig had already signed a contract for his first teaching position, and I asked him what methods he was planning to use in his own social studies classes. He said that he wanted to try different methods, including Jim's storytelling, cooperative learning, and some of the activities he learned in Liza's methods course. I was struck by how closely Craig's answer corresponded to Jim's prediction of what Craig would do in his first year of independent practice: try a number of pedagogical formats—adapting, adopting, or rejecting them depending upon his success with students.

Craig added that, thanks to his experiences with Jim, he acquired a new respect for the importance of teacher-student interaction. He is eager to establish the kind of positive rapport with his students that comes so naturally to Jim.

Betty, Laura's student teacher, took Beth's course on methods of teaching secondary English and was much more critical of her university preparation than was Craig. With the exception of a few grammar lessons that Beth modeled, Betty could cite nothing in the methods course that she felt was relevant to the task of teaching secondary students:

"I learned more about grammar and how to teach it from my first two weeks of student teaching than I did in the entire semester of the methods course."

Having spoken to Beth at length about her emphasis on methods that actually work in secondary classrooms, I found Betty's evaluation of the methods course puzzling. I tried to probe for specific reasons she found Beth's course irrelevant:

"We didn't learn anything about what to expect from high school students or what to do as teachers," she answered. "I had been out of high school for a long time and I felt I needed to get back in touch with students."

It may be significant to note here that at the time Betty took Beth's course, it lacked an observational/clinical component. Since then Beth has inserted one.

The heart of Betty's dissatisfaction with the methods course seemed to be that it gave her no "sense of the students or the reality of teaching." In fact, she could remember Beth alluding only to teaching in college rather than secondary classrooms. As a result Betty was pleasantly surprised by the atmosphere she found at Central High. For the first time in her preservice education, she became "excited and enthusiastic about the prospect of becoming a teacher."

As she became acquainted with Laura's students, Betty also became aware of the darker side of school culture: students' lack of respect for teachers and the desperate home lives with which many must cope. She has seen how family pressures can drive some students to suicidal thoughts and antisocial behaviors in the classroom.

I asked Betty what she learned from Laura that was absent in her university course work: "I learned what high school students are really like and how to win their respect, which I see as a major task of teachers today. I also learned how to handle parent-teacher conferences and how to organize my work."

When Betty gets her own classes next year she plans to model her practice after Laura's: "I see what Mrs. Hunter does as being very effective. Students learn and often get excited about learning. She's fun in class; they respect her; and she helps them put aside their outside problems for a while so they can concentrate on school work."

Betty also spoke of close friends who are completing their student teaching assignments but are having negative experiences. The source of their dissatisfaction seems to be a lack of direct guidance from their respective cooperating teachers. Like Betty, the student teachers feel they were given no concrete information in course work and are now left in a frightening vacuum. Betty also mentioned friends who are now enrolled in Beth's methods course, who phone her several times a week to learn vicariously about students and schools.

What courses, if any, had provided Betty with useful information about teaching and students? She cited a course in educational psychology and another in human development, "because they told me something about the nature of the kids I would be teaching." She also mentioned a six-hour block of course work that entails the only clinical experience for secondary education majors prior to the semester of student teaching. The university-based portion of that block introduced Betty to the general format of a lesson plan and some basic considerations concerning lessons (e.g., the need for a motivating activity, closure, etc.). At least lesson plans were concrete and specific.

The weekend prior to our interview, Betty had taken the National Teacher Examination. She wanted me to know that in answering items on the Professional Knowledge section of the exam she had drawn exclusively from her experiences with Laura. She found nothing in her university course work that was relevant to the questions: "The questions described hypothetical situations and asked you to choose the most appropriate action for a teacher. Since none of my courses discussed realistic classroom experiences, they were of no use. But in working with Mrs. Hunter, I observed or participated in situations similar to those on the test."

In sum, both student teachers saw university course work as being out of touch with the context of contemporary classrooms. Specifically, professors failed to address the nature of today's adolescent students, what to expect from them, and how to win their respect.

According to Craig, Liza had been more successful than Beth in trying to relate pedagogical theory to practice. Nevertheless, I was impressed with the paradox: despite Liza's and Beth's efforts to root their respective courses in the pragmatics of classrooms, many of their students may have failed to see the relevance of their courses to classroom teaching. Yet, by watching Jim and Laura organize material and interact with students, Craig and Betty were apparently able to acquire a wide range of relevant information.

Echoes in the Literature of Teaching and Teacher Education: The Functional Value of Each Perspective

There is nothing surprising about the discrepant views of classroom teaching elicited from the professors and the teachers. Indeed, one can trace these two perspectives through four decades of literature on teaching and teacher education. The differences in perspectives have been explained most frequently in terms of differential "cultures": that is, the socializing effects of two distinctively different workplaces, schools and universities (Brookhart and Loadman, 1990; Lanier and Little, 1986; Zeichner and Gore, 1990; Zeichner, Tabachnick, and Densmore, 1987).

The difference between the two cultures is usually defined in terms of a predilection for the pragmatic (by teachers) as opposed to the theoretical (by professors)—a contradiction often manifested by a cooperating teacher and a university supervisor giving discrepant advice to a student teacher (Feiman-Nemser and Buchmann, 1987). It may be the root of candidates' frequent complaints that there is no connection between what professors teach in university courses and what teachers actually practice in classrooms (Hoy and Woolfolk, 1989; Lanier and Little, 1986; Zeichner, 1990).

However, dismissing the distinction between the two perspectives as the result of socialization merely begs the issue. Cultures are not constructed arbitrarily; in order to truly understand a culture, one must probe the functional values of the beliefs and behaviors associated with it. That is, one must assume there is a rationale beneath the culture of schools that is as coherent and functional as that which underlies the culture of universities. Moreover, to continue characterizing the two perspectives as simply a split between theory and practice is reductive and somewhat misleading. This becomes clear as one examines the implicit and explicit allusions to the two cultures in the literature.

The University View of Classroom Teaching: A Science

Ever since the education of teachers became a business of universities, professors have tried to cast classroom teaching in scientific terms: to construct neat, logical models that account for student learning in terms of theories derived from cognitive psychology. This tendency may have reached its peak during the 1970s, when large-scale process-product studies were conducted in an effort to identify observable teacher behaviors that were statistically associated with student achievement:

> Over the years many people have struggled to "neatinize" teaching, to simplify and define it, and to somehow get control of it. For the past thirty years educational researchers have made large claims for the value of research on teaching. Scientific approaches and process-product designs would herald a new day of understanding and enlightened practice. (Ayers, 1992, p. 148)

However, despite large samples and sophisticated statistics, the search for significant correlates of student achievement was disappointing. The only consistently significant predictor to emerge from these studies was "time-on-task": the amount of classroom time students spent working on academic tasks. Thus, a relatively focused decade of applied research yielded only the self-evident observation that the more instructional time students spend working on academic material, the more they are likely to learn.

In the early 1980 the process-product approach was replaced by a new research paradigm: a search for the cognition underlying expert teaching (Berliner, 1986; Kagan, 1988; Shulman, 1987). This shift altered the university view of teaching in two ways: by moving the focus of study to the nonobservable (rather than the observable) elements of classroom teaching, and by assuming that the naturalistic study of expert teachers could be instructive to researchers.

Research on teacher cognition also represented the beginning of a concerted effort to identify a scientific "knowledge base" that underlies competent teaching. The functional value of such a knowledge base is obvious:

> ...through a claim to a sophisticated knowledge base at a high level, teaching might aspire, like medicine or law, to professional status. By demonstrating a specialised knowledge base that requires several years of study to master, greater importance and status might be attached to the training and licensing of teachers. Secondly, it is presumed that a specific knowledge base underpins the practice of teaching and therefore by defining this knowledge, one is in a better position to prepare student teachers for the teaching task. (Calderhead, 1991, p. 531)

Despite the change in focus and research methodology, contemporary studies of teacher cognition remain decidedly scientific in their rhetoric and ultimate objective: the construction of a neat epistemology of teaching. To date, the most researched and publicized version of such a knowledge base has been explicated by Shulman (1987) and his colleagues at Stanford University. It describes three interrelated bases: content knowledge (of academic material), pedagogical knowledge (of generic teaching strategies and principles), and pedagogical content knowledge (of vehicles and devices a teacher can use to translate content knowledge so students can understand it). In 1989 the American Association of

Colleges for Teacher Education published the first volume of its *Knowledge Base for the Beginning Teacher* (Reynolds, 1989). Chapters draw heavily on the implications of cognitive theory for classroom instruction.

The driving image of contemporary research on teaching is that of the classroom teacher as an expert practitioner (Kagan, 1988; Kennedy, 1987), an image that implies technical know-how (Welker, 1992). In accordance with the technical connotations of expertise, the pedagogical method a teacher employs could be regarded as a "treatment": a scientific manipulation of academic content that causes student learning. In this sense even the most recent research on teaching is dominated implicitly by a sort of "social physics" (Geertz, 1983), a conception of classroom teaching and learning that assumes direct, predictable cause-effect relationships.

In an effort to mitigate the scientific tone of contemporary research on teacher cognition, some researchers now refer to teachers' professional knowledge as "personal theories," "practical knowledge," or "narratives" (Connelly and Clandinin, 1988; Elbaz, 1983). Each of those terms suggests that the knowledge is somewhat more subjective and contextualized than scientific theory. However, even with that qualification, studies of teacher cognition assume scientific explanations and rhetoric.

A fine example of this bias is Clift's (1992) two-year qualitative study of a novice English teacher, Lesley, as she completed her preservice program. To document the cognition of learning to teach, Clift collected a variety of data: transcripts of interviews with Lesley, videotapes and field observations of her teaching during clinical experiences of her program, entries from a journal Lesley was required to keep. Clift analyzed and discussed the data in terms of three problems Lesley encountered during the field components of her program.

Ultimately Clift attributed the problems to the need to integrate knowledge across separate "schemas" that were inherent in the university course work Lesley took. By schemas, Clift means the discrete bodies of knowledge to which Lesley was exposed, knowledge about: literary analysis, the teaching of literature, the teaching of language, assessment and evaluation of student learning, planning for instruction, etc. In conclusion, Clift suggests that in order to function successfully in the classroom, Lesley (and other novices) must interrelate these separate knowledge bases and apply them to specific problems.

However, one can read Clift's (1992) data very differently. Every problem Lesley encountered in classrooms was caused by an insufficient knowledge of pupils and ways to communicate with them. As Clift herself admits, this was the aspect of Lesley's professional knowledge that changed most during her clinical experiences. As Lesley acquired a knowledge of pupils, she used it to mitigate her knowledge of academic material and her image of self-as-teacher.

My point here is that Clift's study is typical of the university bias: the tendency to interpret and discuss classroom data (and teachers' discourse) in terms of cognitive theory (knowledge bases, schemas, etc.) rather than the more obvious terms of student-teacher relationships (the teachers' perspective).

However, a close look at recent learning-to-teach studies tends to confirm the teachers' rather than the professors' perspective. A review of forty studies that documented changes in the beliefs or behaviors of preservice and beginning teachers suggested that learning to teach entails three fundamental tasks: (a) acquiring instructional-management routines; (b) acquiring knowledge of pupils; and (c) using that knowledge to mitigate one's image of self-as-teacher (Kagan, 1992b). In sum, these studies suggest that learning to teach largely amounts to learning how to relate to students—an observation remarkably consistent with the views expressed by Laura and Jim.

Thus, ironically research on teacher cognition has provided some of the most powerful evidence undermining the university perspective, evidence that confirms the view that teaching is *not* a science. Some of these studies are discussed in greater detail below.

The Teachers' View: Teaching as Art

In recent years and in increasing numbers, articles and books on teaching have begun to testify to the opposite perspective: classroom teaching as a highly personalized form of art (e.g., Cohen, 1991; Hargreaves, 1990; Huberman, 1990; Kagan, 1992a; Pratte and Rury, 1991). For example, studies that cut across content fields attest to the atheoretical nature of teachers' professional knowledge (Clark and Peterson, 1986; Duffy, 1977; Harste, 1985; Morine-Dershimer, 1987, 1988; Olson, 1981; Richardson and Hamilton, 1988; Sosniak, Ethington, and Varelas, 1991). A common finding in studies of teacher cognition is that relationships between a teacher's thoughts and classroom practices are not always linear; in fact, teachers often espouse beliefs that actually conflict with their practices (Calderhead, 1991).

One can also find a variety of literature that demonstrates the idiosyncratic and expressive nature of teaching by illustrating the close relationship between the biographies and classroom practices of teachers (e.g., Connelly and Clandinin, 1988; Cohen, 1991; Lightfoot, 1983; Schubert and Ayers, 1992; Wright and Tuska, 1968; Yee, 1990). According to these studies, teachers' professional development appears to be a continual process of self-definition, as teachers express their individuality through their interaction with students and the curriculum (Cole, 1991).

This hypothesis is confirmed by research on attempts to change teachers' classroom practices, which suggests that too much of a teacher's knowledge reflects biography and personality to be amenable to revolutionary change. To influence practice, one must address a teacher's life story, personal beliefs, and prior experiences (Cohen, 1990; Louden, 1991). Thus, "the individual teacher continues to make and remake the classroom based on his or her own imagination, spirit, inspiration, and learning" (Lieberman and Miller, 1991, p. 108).

The highly personal and idiosyncratic nature of teaching is also confirmed by many contemporary learning-to-teach studies illustrating the importance of a novice's image of self-as-teacher (Bullough, 1987, 1990; Bullough and Knowles, 1990; Bullough, Knowles. and Crow, 1989; Strahan, 1990; Wendel, 1989; Wildman, Niles, Magliaro, and McLaughlin, 1989).

Finally, one can find studies that support the notion that the heart of classroom teaching lies in individual student-teacher relationships (Lyons, 1990). Yee's (1990) study of teachers' careers revealed that a large part of the professional expertise teachers acquire over time consists of the ability to "read" and relate to children. As one teacher reflected: "I now have more knowledge of different personalities and how to work with them. I can spot earlier when students need my attention. I can still be fooled by students, but it's not so serious" (Yee, 1990, p. 53). Empirical studies of the classroom cases teachers write (Kagan and Tippins, 1991a) and the ways student teachers describe their pupils (Kagan and Tippins, 1991b) suggest that, in part, learning to teach means becoming sensitive to and affected by the complex, often problematic nature of pupils.

This is not to say that researchers have completely ignored the affective elements of teaching, however, they are regarded as separate from and secondary to the "cognition" of classroom practice (Hargreaves and Tucker, 1991). When researchers do allude to the intuitive and affective elements of teaching, it tends to be in pejorative terms. For example, Book, Byers, and Freeman (1983) found that entering teacher candidates tended to emphasize the interpersonal (rather than the cognitive) aspects of teaching. The researchers promptly warned readers that when teaching is seen as an extension of the kind of nurturing relationship that typifies parenting, teaching is diminished as a profession.

Despite this bias, the teachers' perspective of classroom teaching is appearing more frequently in the scholarly press. A small segment of the university community has even begun to question the validity of a "knowledge base" for teaching:

> It implies that teacher knowledge is extremely rational and highly technical—or that it ought to aspire to be so—rather than being essentially multidimensional and intersub-jective. The list [of knowledge bases] constructs teaching

as orderly, systematic and generalizable, rather than person-specific and circumstantial. It casts teacher knowledge as arcane and inaccessible, something that is primarily generated by outside researchers and experts and then transferred more or less successfully to practitioners. . .Furthermore, any list of teacher knowledge ignores or obscures another, perhaps more urgent consideration: the dispositions of mind that may be required to be an effective or outstanding teacher, dispositions that may be difficult or impossible to teach in a straightforward way. . .(Ayers, 1992, p. 149)

These same scholars point out that the rhetoric and tenets underlying the university perspective present teaching as an objectified subject of academic study and research; they fail to address classroom teaching as it is actually experienced:

> Teaching is found in the actions of everyday practice, the very stuff that is washed away in most attempts to generalize about teaching. To unlock the reality of teaching is to move beyond the distanced and sanitized language of the social scientist, the bloodless objectivity of the technician and the experts. . .and to enter the messy, subjective world of teachers where the talk is idiosyncratic and particular, infused with immediacy and urgently linked to conduct. It is to pierce the veil of facts, and to partake of value-talk and feeling-talk, talk of the ordinary and the mundane, and yet talk that is frequently eloquent, consistently thoughtful, and almost always characterized by an abiding sense of care and connection. (Ayers, 1992, p. 152)

Here we arrive at the functional value of the teachers' view of classroom teaching. When asked to describe their professional knowledge and experiences, seasoned teachers invariably speak or write about specific students and specific student-teacher relationships (Berliner, 1986; Kagan and Tippins, 1991a, 1991b; Leinhardt, 1990; Yee, 1990). Moreover, the primacy of student-teacher relationships (as opposed to pedagogical method) has emerged as a consistent theme in studies and surveys of both pre- and inservice teachers (e.g., Cohn and Kottkamp, 1993; Hollingsworth, Teel, and Minarik, 1992; Little, 1992; Schlosser, 1992). In short, this appears to be the idiom of experience: the perspective teachers use to understand, explain, and evaluate what they do in classrooms. It is the teachers' perspective (Table 8.1) that is *consistent with and indigenous to* the way classroom teaching is lived on a daily basis.

One could logically infer that it must also be the most appropriate perspective for educating teachers-in-training. Perhaps the reason most university course work in preservice programs is regarded by candidates as irrelevant is that professors use a perspective that is inconsistent with the lived experience of teaching. Beth and Liza undoubtedly had a great deal of useful information to contribute to the education of their methods students, but they may have couched it in nonfunctional terms. To contribute to the preservice education of teachers, professors may need to acknowledge the teachers' perspective and to speak, not in terms of a science of pedagogy, but in terms of student-teacher relationships.

Summary

One could undoubtedly find good classroom teachers whose pedagogical beliefs do not match Jim's and Laura's. As I explained initially, one of my reasons for selecting Jim and Laura was their traditional, teacher-centered styles. However, four decades of research suggest there are many other outstanding teachers with similar beliefs and practices. The same could be said of Beth and Liza as representatives of the community of education professors.

Inferences and Implications

The Preservice Education of Teachers

One of the clearest implications of this project is that traditional programs of preservice teacher education are inappropriate, because they are based on the university perspective. As such, they are designed to provide novices with technical information about pedagogical methods derived insight to give to teachers-in-training (this might also explain why the process-product search for correlates of student achievement failed). As others have noted, we do not possess a psychology of human relationships, much less a psychology of classroom interaction (Hartup and Rubin, 1986; Hinde, 1979; Lyons, 1990). The closest we come are studies of teacher expectation and perception which were part of the process-product era (Brophy and Good, 1974; Cooper, 1979; Good and Brophy, 1973; Levine and Wang, 1983). *Knowledge Base for the Beginning Teacher* (Reynolds, 1989) is notably silent on the issue of student-teacher rapport.

Where We Might Go from Here: The Moral of the Story

I began this book with a description of an argument between Jim and me. In truth, I have had many more arguments with my university colleagues, many of whom see the two perspectives of classroom teaching in terms of "right" and "wrong." Many professors of education have told me why most classroom teachers, because they don't teach the right way (according to the tenets of constructivism) and are unfamiliar with educational research, are unqualified to make important decisions about preservice education.

Most contemporary classroom research is not only written by education professors but explicitly assumes that their perspective is more correct than that of classroom teachers (e.g., Cobb, Wood, Yackel, and McNeal, 1992; Sinatra, Beck, and McKeown, 1992; Stein, Baxter, and Leinhardt, 1990). Indeed, many studies may be viewed as thinly disguised prescriptive tracts (e.g., Brophy, 1992).

Like Liza and Beth, professors of education usually attribute teachers' adherence to the "wrong" pedagogical methods to ignorance or external constraints. For example, Cohn and Kottkamp (1993), professors who are generally sympathetic to the plight of classroom teachers, explained the persistence of teacher-centered instruction in the following terms:

The fundamental controls of the stable system, with or without the additional legislated layers, serve to constrain both teachers and students from working in more individualized, active, and student-centered ways...teachers have historically relied on a teacher-centered model because it is a practical accommodation to the existing teacher-student ratio and the organizational structure of schools.

Finally, we believe that the vast majority of teachers would maintain that even if they could positively confront the discomfort that would accompany a major shift from external to internal controls and a shift from teacher- to student-centered pedagogy, they would not have the knowledge or skill to do it. (Cohn and Kottkamp, 1993, p. 243–244).

That explanation is inconsistent with Jim's contention that his colleagues are familiar with indirect and inductive pedagogical models, but prefer to use teacher-centered instruction, because it is more effective. Unfortunately, good traditional teachers like Laura and Jim remain politely silent on this and other issues—part of an underground of practitioners that sees the products of nonfunctional programs of preservice teacher education.

If there is a moral to this story, it is that professors and teachers must learn to respect the functional values of each others' perspectives, which I have summarized in Table 8.2. These functional values suggest *the reasons why* teachers and professors may have come to endorse their respective views. For university professors, casting teaching in terms of scientific theory allows them to compete academically with professors in the other disciplines one finds on university campuses: that is, it allows them to conduct and publish research that conforms to the format of the social sciences (which is patterned after that of the hard sciences). It allows them to ignore the artistic and idiosyncratic elements of teaching that, if acknowledged, would put the profession of teaching far down on the epistemological peeking order—equivalent to an art rather than a science (Schon, 1987).

For classroom teachers, describing teaching in terms of human relationships and interaction may be most compatible

To generate such research, a researcher may need to function as I did during this project: as a collaborator whose job includes asking experienced teachers questions, confronting them with written transcripts of their responses, and helping them explore the rationale underlying their practice. That is not the hard part, for researchers of teacher cognition have already grown accustomed to playing the role of collaborator.

The part researchers may have difficulty accepting is then *refraining from translating teachers' discourse into scientific theory*, as Clift (1992) did with Lesley's discourse. As impressive as cognitive theories and the jargon of epistemology may sound, my colleagues may have to acknowledge that they represent an incestuous enterprise that (a) does not accurately reflect the lived experience of classroom teaching, and (b) is not a functional idiom for educating preservice candidates.

When I suggested this to a good friend who is a professor of education at a major research university in the United States, she disagreed strongly, pointing out that many of the classroom teachers who work regularly with professors on her campus are manifesting great changes in their pedagogical beliefs and practices: that is, they are abandoning traditional, teachers centered, information-giving formats for pedagogical methods more compatible with constructivism. She also cited the increasingly popular phenomenon of the professional development school as a powerful vehicle for transmuting the culture of schools.

I have no doubt that such a transformation will occur in many cases, if for no other reason than because of the disproportionate amount of status associated with university as opposed to school culture (Brookhart and Loadman, 1990). If classroom teachers have learned one lesson well, it is that their views are without value compared to the discourse of education professors. But I would like my colleagues in colleges of education to consider the possibility that ours may be a Pyrrhic victory: that in converting teachers to our way of thinking, we may be losing an equally valid and valuable source of insight about the human mind and spirit. To preserve a valuable source of insight, we may have to "learn to walk in different ways, to converse in new languages, to listen to different voices, to care. . ." (Day, 1991, p. 546).

To illustrate how different the rhetoric of professors and classroom teachers can be, I have juxtaposed samples of discourse in Table 8.3. Where one community of practitioners cites theory and pedagogical method, the other talks about children and the texture of human relationships.

How realistic is it to expect professors of education to acknowledge such things? It would require them to relinquish some of the power they now monopolize: that is, the power to explain and proscribe teaching and the power to decide how novices are to be educated. Some may regard this as a naive expectation, but in a year when we have seen the Iron Curtain rise and the Berlin Wall fall, it does not seem too much to ask of two well-meaning communities of educators, both of which claim to have the best interests of children at heart.

Table 8.3

Comparing the Rhetoric of Professors with the Rhetoric of Classroom Teachers

Professors of education talking about classroom teaching	*Classroom teachers talking about teaching*
. . .discourse that indicates knowledge of social studies content requires the student to integrate relevant formal knowledge of the field into one's own language by referring to proper names and authoritative explanations or interpretations. But these must be produced as responses to novel, contextualized problems that challenge the student to use knowledge in new ways. In short, the questions must invite the production of contextualized knowledge by the student rather than the mechanistic reproduction of isolated knowledge bits removed from social context. (Newmann, 1992, p. 54)	Primary kids are little, but they love to finish tasks; they are very task-oriented. They love to check things off that they've done. And I used to have spots in the room where when they finished something, they could get up out of their seat, walk over there, and mark it down. . .I don't really think that the high school kids are much different from that. They like to have a sense of accomplishing something, finishing something, going from one task to another. . .(Millies, 1992, p. 39)
	If you really put yourself in a child's place, then you're coming from where that child is into the strange environment of school. But if you're coming from your own perspective as a teacher, then *you* are comfortable. (Melnick, 1992, p. 89)
When we talk science, we are helping to create, or re-create, a community of people who share certain beliefs and values. We communicate best with people who are already members of our own community: those who have learned to use language in the same ways that we do. . .Science teachers belong to a community of people who already speak the language of science. Students, at least for a long time, do not. Teachers use that language to make sense of each topic in a particular	The children keep me going. For example, one little boy entered an oratory contest. I gave him a black poem which was written in black dialect. I helped him practice. He won first place, and I was just so elated. (Melnick, 1992, p. 89)

Table 8.3 (cont.)

Comparing the Rhetoric of Professors with the Rhetoric of Classroom Teachers

Professors of education talking about classroom teaching	*Classroom teachers talking about teaching*
way. Students use their own language to put together a view of the subject that can be very different. This is one reason why communicating science can be so difficult. We have to learn to see science teaching as a social process and to bring students, at least partially, into this community of people who talk science (Lemke, 1990, p. x.) The belief that we first engage in the simple process of acquiring knowledge bits and later learn the more complex process of using them has been increasingly challenged by cognitive science. Instead, acquisition, storage, retrieval, application, and synthesis can be seen as simultaneous, interactive processes. (Newmann, 1992, p. 59)	I am teaching people who know absolutely nothing about my subject, so it's up to me to say, "Here is what you should learn in order to become more educated. If you use these disciplines I'm imparting to you, your mind will be better. If you don't, it won't." Education is the transfer of information as well as the technique of how to use it. A good teacher teaches not only what a noun is, but how a noun functions in a sentence. Now, in order to teach a kid what a noun is, I have to have him memorize certain things about grammar. It's a rote operation having nothing to do with his enlightenment...In other words, first you learn the tools for perception—an arduous and dull process. Then the capacity to reason begins. Then everything opens up. But I bet that most of the things you do when you start thinking go back to something that's internally structured in your head through the process of rote recitation. There's a very important place in education for that...Now, a progressive educator would say I'm killing creativity...What I'm doing is teaching them discipline, and it's from discipline that creativity comes. (Cohen, 1991, p. 38)

REFERENCES

Ashton, P. T., and Webb, R. B. 1986. *Making a difference: Teachers' sense of efficacy and student achievement.* New York: Longman.

Ayers, W. 1992. Keeping them variously: Learning from the bees themselves. In W. H. Schubert and W. C. Ayers, eds. *Teacher Lore* (pp. 148–53). New York: Longman.

Beach, R., and Marshall, J. 1991. *Teaching literature in the secondary school.* New York: Harcourt Brace Jovanovich.

Berliner, D. C. 1986. In pursuit of the expert pedagogue. *Educational Researcher* 15(7): 5–13.

Book, C.; Byers, J.; and Freeman, D. 1983. Student expectations and teacher education traditions with which we cannot live. *Journal of Teacher Education* 34: 30–51.

Bransford, J. D., and Vye, N. J. 1989. A perspective on cognitive research and its implications for instruciton. In L. B. Resnick and L. E. Klopfer, eds. *Toward the thinking curriculum* (1989 Yearbook of the Association for Supervision and Curriculum Development, pp. 173–205). Alexandria, Va.: Association for Supervision and Curriculum Development.

Brookhart, S. M., and Loadman, W. E. 1990. Empirical evidence that school-university collaboration is multicultural education. *Teaching and Teacher Education* 6: 149–63.

Brophy, J., ed. 1992. *Advances in research on teaching, vol. 3: Planning and managing learning tasks and activities.* Greenwich, CT.: JAI Press.

Brophy, J. E., and Good, T. L. 1974. *Teacher-student relationships: Causes and consequences*. New York: Holt, Rinehart, and Winston.

Bullough, R. V. 1987. Planning and the first year of teaching. *Journal of Education for Teaching* 13: 231–50.

Bullough, R. V. 1989. *First year teacher: A case study*. New York: Teachers College Press.

Bullough, R. V., Jr. 1990. Supervision, mentoring, and self-discovery: A case study of a first-year teacher. *Journal of Curriculum and Supervision* 5: 338–60.

Bullough, R. V., and Knowles, J. G. 1990. Becoming a teacher: Struggles of a second-career beginning teacher. *Qualitative Studies in Education* 3: 101–12.

Bullough, R. V.; Knowles, J. G.; and Crow, N. A. 1989. Teacher self-concept and student culture in the first year of teaching. *Teachers College Records* 91: 209–33.

Calderhead, J. 1988. The contribution of field experience to primary student teachers' professional learning. *Research in Education* 40: 33–49.

Calderhead, J. 1991. The nature and growth of knowledge in student teaching. *Teaching and Teacher Education* 7: 531–35.

Carr, W., and Kemmis, S. 1986. *Becoming critical: Education, knowledge, and action research*. London: Falmer.

Clark, B. R. 1987. *The academic life: Small worlds, different worlds*. Princeton, N.J.: Carnegie Foundation.

Clark, C. M., and Peterson, P. L. 1986. Teachers' thought processes. In M. C. Wittrock, ed. *Handbook of research on teaching* (3d ed., pp. 255–96). New York: Macmillan.

Clift. R. T. 1992. Learning to teach English—maybe: A study of knowledge development. *Journal of Teacher Education* 42(5): 357–72.

Cobb, P., Wood, T., Yackel, E., and McNeal, B. 1992. Characteristics of classroom mathematics traditions: An interactional anaysis. *American Eduational Research Journal* 29: 573–604.

Cohen. D. K. 1990. A revolution in one classroom: The case of Mrs. Oublier. *Educational Evaluation and Policy Analysis* 12: 311–30.

Cohen, R. M. 1991. *A lifetime of teaching: Portraits of five veteran high school teachers.* New York: Teachers College Press.

Cohn, M. M., and Kottkamp, R. B. 1993. *Teachers: The missing voice in education.* Albany: State University of New York Press.

Cole, A. L. 91. Relationships in the workplace: Doing what comes naturally? *Teaching and Teacher Education* 7: 415–26.

Connelly, F. M., and Clandinin, D. J. 1988. *Teachers as curriculum planners: Narratives of experience.* New York: Teachers College Press.

Cooper, H. M. 1979. Pygmalion grows up: A model for teacher expectation, communication and performance influence. *Review of Educational Research* 49: 389–410.

Cuban, L. 1993. *How teachers taught.* New York: Teachers College Press.

Day, C. 1991. Roles and relationships in qualitative research on teachers' thinking: A reconsideration. *Teaching and Teacher Education* 7: 537–47.

Duffy, G. 1977, December. *A study of teacher conceptions of reading.* Paper presented at the National Reading Conference, New Orleans.

Eisner, E. W. 1991. *The enlightened eye: Qualitative injuiry and the enhancement of educational practice.* New York: Macmillan.

Elbaz, F. 1983. *Teacher thinking: A study of practical knowledge.* New York: Nichols.

Feimen-Nemser, S., and Buchmann, M. 1987. When is student teaching teacher education? *Teaching and Teacher Education* 3: 255–74.

Feiman-Nemser, S., and Floden, R. E. 1986. The cultures of teaching. In W. C. Wittrock., ed. *Handbook of research on teaching* (3d ed., pp. 505–26). New York: Macmillan.

Geertz, C. 1983. *Local knowledge: Further essays in interpretive anthropology.* New York: Basic Books.

Good, T. L., and Brophy, J. E. 1973. *Looking into classrooms.* New York: Harper and Row.

Goodman, K. 1986. *What's whole in whole languages?* Portsmouth, N.H.: Heinemann.

Hall, G. E., and Loucks, S. F. 1982. Bridging the gap: Policy research rooted in practice. In A. Lieberman and M. W. McLaughlin, eds. *Policy making in education* (81st Yearbook of the National Society for the Study of Education, Part I, pp. 133–58). Chicago: University of Chicago Press.

Hargreaves, A. 1990, April. *Individualism and individuality: Reinterpreting the culture of teaching.* Paper presented at the annual meeting of the American Educational Research Association, Boston.

Hargreaves, A., and Tucker, E. 1991. Teaching and guilt: Exploring the feelings of teachers. *Teaching and Teacher Education* 7: 491–505.

Harste, J. C. 1985. Portrait of a new paradigm: Reading comprehension research. In A. Crismore, ed. *Landscapes: A state-of-the-art assessment of reading comprehension research. 1974–1984* (pp. 1–24). Bloomington, IN.: Indiana University.

Hartup, W., and Rubin, Z., eds. 1986. *Relationships and development.* Hillsdale, N.J.: Lawrence Erlbaum.

Hinde, R. A. 1979. *Towards understanding relationships.* London: Academic Press.

Hollingsworth, S. 1989. Prior beliefs and cognitive change in learning to teach. *American Educational Research Journal* 26: 160–89.

Hollingsworth, S., Teel, K., and Minarik, L. 1992. Learning to teach Aaron: A beginning teacher's story of literacy instruction in an urban classroom. *Journal of Teacher Education* 43(2): 116–27.

The Holmes Group 1986. *Tomorrow's teachers.* East Lansing, MI: Holmes Group.

Hoy, W. K. 1969. Pupil control ideology and organizational socialization: A further examination of the influence of experience on the beginning teacher. *School Review* 77: 257–65.

Hoy, W. K., and Woolfolk, A. E. 1989. Supervising student teachers. In A. E. Woolfolk, ed. *Research perspectives on the graduate education of teachers* (pp. 108–31). Englewood Cliffs, N.J.: Prentice-Hall.

Huberman, A. 1990, April. *The model of independent artisan in teachers' professional relations.* Paper presented at the annual metting of the Ameican Educational Research Association, Boston.

Kagan. D. M. 1988. Teaching as clinical problem solving: A critical examination of the analogy and its implications. *Review of Educational Research* 58: 482–505.

Kagan, D. M. 1992a. Implications of research on teacher belief. *Educational Psychologist* 27: 65–90.

Kagan, D. M. 1992b. Professional growth among preservice and beginning teachers. *Review of Educational Research* 62: 129–69.

Kagan, D. M., and Tippins, D. J. 1991a. How teachers' classroom cases express their pedagogical beliefs. *Journal of Teacher Education* 42(4): 281–91.

Kagan, D. M., and Tippins, D. J. 1991b. How student teachers describe their pupils. *Teaching and Teacher Education* 7: 455–66.

Kennedy, M. 1987. Inexact sciences: Professional education and the development of expertise. *Review of Research in Education* 14: 133–67.

Kirman, J. M. 1988. Integrating geography with other school subjects. *Journal of Geography* 87: 104–6.

Labaree, D. F. 1992. Power, knowledge, and the rationalization of teaching: A geneology of the movement to professionalize teaching. *Harvard Educational Review* 62: 123–54.

Lanier, J. E., and Little, J. W. 1986. Research on teacher education. In M. C. Wittrock, ed. *Handbook of research on teaching.* (3d ed., pp. 527–69). New York: Macmillan.

Leinhardt, G. 1990. Capturing craft knowledge in teaching. *Educational Researcher* 19: 18–25.

Lemke, J. L. 1990. *Talking science: Language, learning, and values.* Norwood, N.J.: Ablex.

Levine, J. M., and Wang, M. C., 1983. *Teacher and student perceptions: Implications for learning.* Hillsdale, N.J.: Lawrence Eribaum.

Lieberman, A., and Miller, L. 1991. Revisiting the social realities of teaching. In A. Lieberman and L. Miller, eds. *Staff development for education in the 90's* (2d ed., pp. 92–112). New York: Teachers College Press.

Lightfoot, S. L. 1983. The lives of teachers. In L. S. Shulman and G. Sykes, eds. *Handbook of teaching and policy* (pp. 241–60). New York: Longman.

Little, W. 1992. Opening the black box of professional community. In A. Lieberman, ed. *The changing contexts of teaching* (91st Yearbook of the National Society for the Study of Education, Part 1, pp. 157–178). Chicago: University of Chicago Press.

Louden, W. 1991. *Understanding teaching: Continuity and change in teachers' knowledge.* New York: Teachers College Press.

Lyons, N. 1990. Epistemological dimensions of teachers' work and development. *Harvard Educational Reviews* 60: 159–80.

Lytle, S. L., and Cochran-Smith, M. 1991. *Teacher research as a way of knowing.* Unpublished manuscript.

Magliaro, S. G.; Wildman, T. M.; Niles, J. A.; McLaughlin, R. A.; and Ferro, S. 1989, March. *Modeling the transition from novice to expert: A three-year study of teacher problem solving.* Paper presented at the annual meeting of the American Educational Research Association, San Francisco.

Melnick, C. R. 1992. The out-of-school curriculum: An invitation, not an inventory. In W. H. Schubert and W. C. Ayers, eds. *Teacher Lore* (pp. 81–106). New York: Longman.

Merseth, K. K. 1991. *The case for cases in teacher education.* Washington, D.C.: American Association for Higher Education and American Association of Colleges for Teacher Education.

Millies, P. S. G. 1992. The relationship between a teacher's life and teaching. In W. H. Schubert and W. C. Ayers, eds. *Teacher lore* (pp. 25–43). New York: Longman.

Morine-Dershimer, G. 1987. Practical examples of the practical argument: A case in point. *Educational Theory* 37: 395–407.

Morine-Dershimer, G. 1988. Premises in the practical arguments of preservice teachers. *Teaching and Teacher Education* 4: 215–29.

Newmann, F. M. 1992. The assessment of discourse in social studies. In H. Berlak, F. M. Newmann, E. Adams, and D. Archbald, *Toward a new science of educational testing and assessment* (pp. 53–70). Albany: State University of New York Press.

Olson, J. K. 1991. Teacher influence in the classroom. *Instructional Sciences* 10: 259–75.

Perl, S. 1980. Understanding composing. *College Composition and Communication* 31: 363–69.

Pratte, R., and Rury, J. L. 1991. Teachers, professionalism, and craft. *Teachers College Record* 93: 59–72.

Resnick, L. B., and Klopfer, L. E. 1989. Toward the thinking curriculum: An overview. In L. B. Resnick and L. E. Klopfer, eds. *Toward the thinking curriculum* (1989 Yearbook of the Association for Supervision and Curriculum Development, pp. 1–18). Alexandria, Va.: Association for Supervision and Curriculum Development.

Reynolds, M. C., ed. 1989. *Knowledge base for the beginning teacher.* New York: Pergamon.

Richardson, V. 1990. Significant and worthwhile change in teaching practice. *Educational Researcher* 19(7): 10–18.

Richardson, V., and Hamilton, M. L. 1988, April. *Teachers' theories of reading.* Paper presented at the annual meeting of the American Educational Research Association, New Orleans.

Rosenholtz, S. J. 1989. *Teachers' workplace: The social organization of schools.* New York: Longman.

Schlosser, L. K. 1992. Teacher distance and student disengagement: School lives on the margin. *Journal of Teacher Education* 43(2): 128–40.

Schon, D. A. 1987. The crisis of professional knowledge and the pursuit of an epistemology of practice. In C. R. Christensen, *Teaching and the case method* (pp. 241–53). Boston: Harvard Business School.

Schubert, W. H., and Ayers, W. C., eds. 1992. *Teacher lore.* New York: Longman.

Shulman, L. S. 1986. Those who understand: Knowledge growth in teaching. *Educational Researcher* 15(2): 4–14.

Shulman, L. S. 1987. Knowledge and teaching: Foundations of the new reform. *Harvard Educational Review* 57: 1–22.

Sinatra, G. M., Beck, I. L., and McKeown, M. G. 1992. A longitudinal characterization of young students' knowledge of their country's government. *American Educational Research Journal* 29: 633–61.

Smylie, M. A. 1989. Teachers' views of the effectiveness of sources of learning to teach. *Elementary School Journal* 89: 543–58.

Sosniak, L. A.; Ethington, C. A.; and Varelas, M. 1991. Teaching mathematics without a coherent point of view. *Journal of Curriculum Studies* 23: 119–31.

Stein, M. K., Baxter, J. A., and Leinhardt, G. 1990. Subject-matter knowledge and elementary instruction: A case from functions and graphing. *American Educational Research Journal* 27: 639–63.

Strahan, D. B. 1990, April. *A developmental analysis of preservice teachers' orientations towards themselves, their students, and their subject matter.* Paper presented at the annual meeting of the American Educational Research Association, Boston.

Tchudi, S. N., and Tchudi, S. J. 1991. *The English/language arts handbook.* Portsmouth, N.H.: Boynton/Cook.

Welker, R. 1992. *The teacher as expert.* Albany: State University of New York Press.

Wendel, R. 1989, March. *A longitudinal study of beginning secondary teachers' decision making from planning through instruction.* Paper presented at the annual meeting of the American Educational Research Association, San Francisco.

Wildman, T. M., Niles, J. A., Magliaro, S. G., and LcLaughlin, R. A. 1989. Teaching and learning to teach: The two roles of beginning teachers. *Elementary School Journal* 89: 471–93.

Wisniewski, R., and Ducharme, E. R., eds. 1989. *The Professors of teaching: An inquiry.* Albany: State University of New York Press.

Wright, B. D., and Tuska, S. A. 1968. From dream to life in the psychology of becoming a teacher. *School Review* 76: 253–93.

Yee, S. M. 1990. *Careers in the classroom.* New York: Teachers College Press.

Zahorik, J. A. 1987. Teachers' collegial interactions: An exploratory study. *Elementary School Journal* 87: 385–96.

Zeichner, K. M. 1990. Changing directions in the practicum: Looking ahead to the 1990s. *Journal of Education for Teaching* 16: 105–32.

Zeichner, K. M., and Gore, J. M. 1990. Teacher socialization. In W. R. Houston, ed. *Handbook of research on teacher education* (pp. 329–48). New York: Macmillan.

Zeichner, K. M.; Tabachnick, B. R.; and Densmore, K. 1987. Individual, institutional, and cultural influences on the development of teachers' craft knowledge. In J. Calderhead, ed. *Exploring teachers' thinking* (pp. 21–59). London: Cassell.

INDEX